Welcome to the won
Regency Ron
For a free short story and to listen to the first chapter of all my other Regencies,
please go to my website or use the QR code:

https://romancenovelsbyglrobinson.com

Thank you!

GL Robinson

Beatrix, the Baron, and His Dog

A Regency Romance
By
GL Robinson

©GL Robinson 2022. All Rights Reserved.

As always, in memory of my dear sister,
Francine.

With thanks to my Beta Readers,
Especially Beryl McMillan, who had her doubts about
chapter 16!
With special thanks to CS for his patient editing and
technical help,
and more especially, for his friendship.

Cover: Thérèse Schwartze, Dutch (1851–1918)

Contents

Chapter One	1
Chapter Two	7
Chapter Three	13
Chapter Four	17
Chapter Five	21
Chapter Six	25
Chapter Seven	35
Chapter Eight	43
Chapter Nine	53
Chapter Ten	59
Chapter Eleven	65
Chapter Twelve	69
Chapter Thirteen	75
Chapter Fourteen	79
Chapter Fifteen	83
Chapter Sixteen	89
Chapter Seventeen	95
Chapter Eighteen	101
Chapter Nineteen	105
Chapter Twenty	111
Chapter Twenty-One	119
Chapter Twenty-Two	125
Chapter Twenty-Three	129
Chapter Twenty-Four	135
Chapter Twenty-Five	139
Chapter Twenty-Six	143
Chapter Twenty-Seven	149
Chapter Twenty-Eight	155

Chapter Twenty-Nine	159
Chapter Thirty	163
Chapter Thirty-One	169
Chapter Thirty-Two	173
Chapter Thirty-Three	177
Chapter Thirty-Four	181
Chapter Thirty-Five	185
Chapter Thirty-Six	189
Chapter Thirty-Seven	193
Chapter Thirty-Eight	199
Chapter Thirty-Nine	203
Chapter Forty	207
Chapter Forty-One	211
Chapter Forty-Two	217
Chapter Forty-Three	221
Chapter Forty-Four	225
Chapter Forty-Five	229
Chapter Forty-Six	233
Chapter Forty-Seven	237
Chapter Forty-Eight	241
Chapter Forty-Nine	245
Regency Novels by GL Robinson	249

Chapter One

"Who is that good-looking lady over there?" Trixie Shelby indicated a matron in the corner. It was late in the Season and rare to see anyone new in town.

"That's the Baroness von Schwerin," said her friend Cornelius Wolfson. A very popular young man-about-town and friends with everybody who knew anything, he was always abreast of the latest *on-dits*. "She's English but her husband was Baron of some unpronounceable place. One of the German States. Anyway, he died and she apparently decided to come home. Her son is somewhere out of town arranging something or other."

This was typical of Cornelius, who knew the main idea of a lot of things but never listened closely enough to anything to get the details.

Trixie looked again at the Baroness. Her hair, between silver and blond, was simply dressed, drawn into the nape of her neck, and as she turned her head to address her neighbor, shown to be held by a fine diamond clip. The whole gave her an old-fashioned, almost regal, appearance which was enhanced by the equally fine diamond drops in her ears and at her smooth throat.

Her gown, likewise, gave her an appearance that was out of the ordinary. Its grey color proclaimed her a widow just out of mourning and while it was not in the current mode, its cut made it far from dowdy. The bodice was low enough to reveal a glimpse of her womanly charms, but not so low as to be unsuitable for a woman in her situation and of her age. When she stood up presently, it was seen to fit to a waist that was still sufficiently slim, with the soft fullness of the skirts beginning below the hips and dropping elegantly to the floor. She was of average height only, but her carriage made her appear taller.

But Cornelius's attention was already elsewhere. "That must be her daughter next to her. Rather pretty, don't you think?"

Trixie had noticed the young lady she took to be the daughter. She was very fair and, as Cornelius had said, rather pretty. Like her mother, she did not look exactly unmodish, but there was something foreign about her. For one thing, her hair was braided around her head, in marked contrast to the prevailing London fashion, which called for hair to be styled on top of the head with falling side curls. From what one could see of her gown, it was rather like her mother's and in a shade of rose that was most becoming. She was sitting ramrod straight. She noticed Trixie looking at her and smiled slightly.

"Who do you know who can introduce me?" said Trixie. "I'd like to meet the Baroness, and her daughter looks as if she could do with a friend."

"As a matter of fact, my mother met her at some get-together of old tabbies the other day. That's how I know about her. Mama is over there. Looks like she's been buttonholed by that bore Bunny Smythe. She'll be glad to be rescued. Come on, and we'll ask her to do the honors."

"Sir, your most obedient," said Cornelius to the Honorable Beaufort Smythe, known to all as Bunny. He was a vacuous gentleman of indeterminate age, known to fasten onto anyone who didn't see him coming, and talk endlessly about his horses. "You won't mind if we talk to my Mama for a moment. Trixie has something she needs to ask her. You know Lady Beatrix, of course."

"Of course." Bunny executed a somewhat graceless bow in her direction, and Trixie curtsied. Then, to their combined relief, he nodded to Cornelius's Mama, mumbled something, and wandered off to look for his next victim.

"Thank God you rescued me, Corny," said his mother. "If I had to hear another word about his successes at Tattersall's this last month I swear I should have forgotten my manners and yawned out loud. It's proof positive that one should leave London at the end of the Season. The company is so thin, one is forced to talk to just anybody. Good evening, Trixie."

Mrs. Wolfson looked at her rather narrowly, for, while she liked Trixie, she was afraid of Cornelius becoming too fond of her. She by no means considered Lady Beatrix a suitable wife for her only son. He was inclined to lack steadiness, and Trixie, with her often excessive liveliness, would do him no good at all.

"Mama, Trixie would like to be presented to the Baroness von Schwerin and her daughter. You'll do the honors, won't you?"

Only too happy to have her son make the acquaintance of any other suitable girl, Mrs. Wolfson stood up with alacrity. They followed her across the room and were soon standing before their quarry.

"Dear Baroness," said Corny's mother, "please allow me to present the Lady Beatrix Shelby, and this is my son Cornelius. Beatrix, Cornelius, this is the Baroness von Schwerin."

Trixie curtsied and Corny made the bow for which he was justly famous. The widow inclined her head kindly and said in a pleasant, low voice with no trace of a foreign accent, "I'm delighted to meet you both. This is my daughter Margarethe. She will be glad to meet someone of her own age. I fear she is finding it dreadfully dull sitting next to her Mama."

"Mama, you know that is not true!" protested the young lady. "I am finding much entertainment in looking at all the people and the fashions."

Though she had only a trace of an accent, what made her sound foreign was that she spoke with a precision that was entirely un-English.

"Have you been in London long, Miss von Schwerin?" asked Trixie.

"Only about two weeks, Lady Beatrix," replied Margarethe.

"Oh, call me Trixie, please, everyone does. And Cornelius is Corny."

"I have no, what do you call it, *pet name*, but you may call me Margaret, if you wish."

"Oh, no," exclaimed Trixie. "*Margarethe* with the *tuh* at the end is so much more unusual. Much better than plain Margaret! If you've only been here two weeks, Margarethe, I imagine everything must still seem strange to you. I hope we will be able to make you feel more at home. The Season is nearly over, but there's still enough going on to keep you entertained."

"Thank you! I know little of this Season you speak of, but there are so many things I should like to see! The museums! The galleries! That is something we did not have at home."

Trixie's taste ran more to the wild animal shows of Astley's Amphitheatre and the exotic trifles one could purchase for pennies at the Pantheon Bazaar, but she did not say so. Instead, though she knew nearly nothing about them, she said, "The Elgin Marbles are, I believe, well worth a visit."

"Ah, yes! Though there is some dispute, is there not, as to the legitimacy of Lord Elgin's claim to the antiquities?"

"I'm afraid I'm not well informed on these matters," said Trixie in some desperation, and changed the subject. "The parks are pretty at the moment, with the trees on the turn. Perhaps we might take a drive one day?"

"Oh yes!" Margarethe clasped her hands together. "Mama and I adore to drive in nature. It was one of our favorite activities at home. We lived in the country, you see."

"Well, I'm not sure you can call the London parks the country," laughed Trixie, "but they're better than the streets, I suppose. If you are free tomorrow at three," she continued in her impulsive way, "my uncle and I will collect you both. He's my guardian, you know. He will be delighted to make your acquaintance and is always looking for an excuse to exercise his horses. If you will give me your direction."

Trixie withdrew a little note pad and gold topped pencil from her reticule and their respective information was exchanged. They continued to converse for a few more moments and then parted, all sides well satisfied. The Baroness and Margarethe were happy to have expanded their London acquaintance, Cornelius was always glad to meet another pretty girl, and Trixie considered she had done well. *The Baroness is perfect*, she said to herself. *Sensible and not addicted to jollification. Now if only I can get Uncle Leonard to recognize it.* Then, wrinkling her nose she thought, *and as for Margarethe, she'll do very well for Corny. He needs a steadying influence. What fun it will be to arrange it all!*

Chapter Two

Lady Beatrix Shelby had lost both her parents in an unfortunate accident when she was a young child and now lived with her Uncle Leonard. But far from living with a constant sense of loss, Trixie could barely remember her mother, and her father not at all. Trixie's father, the Earl of Westhampnet, had been the eldest of three sons of whom her uncle Leonard was the youngest.

Trixie was an only child and there being no male heir, upon the Earl's death, his title and estates had naturally fallen to the second son, Harold, her other uncle. He now lived with his wife and family in the family seat in Hertfordshire. It had been suggested that Lady Beatrix be placed there, but the newly elevated Countess, adopting an air of fatigue that was to become her permanent demeanor whenever she was asked to do something she didn't want, declared herself too exhausted to take on her niece.

"How can I?" she said in failing tones, "with my own boy just a year older than Trixie and the baby still in my arms."

Not that the baby, a daughter named Mariah, was often in her arms. That exhausted her too.

Trixie had therefore gone to her Uncle Leonard as an interim measure, but since his sister-in-law's exhaustion showed no sign of abating, he ended up becoming her permanent guardian. As Trixie's natural exuberance and tendency to flout convention increasingly manifested itself, the indolent Countess congratulated herself on a lucky escape.

The Honorable Leonard Shelby had more heart than sense, and loved and spoiled the young Lady Beatrix from the day she came into his home. Consequently, she cheerfully ran rough-shod over him and the nurse who was her first teacher. Her determined demands were met before she had the need to stamp her little foot, and it was only because she was at heart a good girl that she avoided becoming a complete hellion.

It was her godmother Lady March who found the young Lady Beatrix altogether too indulged and recommended a stern governess. Her uncle found a series of ladies who had tried to perform that duty. They had come and gone with rapidity, unable to deal with the young Trixie's constant questioning, constant demand for activity and constant inattention to her lessons.

But then he found Miss Hester Wood. She by no means answered the description of stern governess. She was not imposing physically, being small and thin; her voice was soft and her disposition retiring. She had been routinely run over by the previous children in her charge and exasperated parents had found her quite useless. They didn't understand that if they could not control their children, a governess was unlikely to be able to do so. Miss Wood was by then in late middle age and had despaired of finding a comfortable position.

But it was her very submissiveness that made her a good companion for the vivacious young lady. She never tried to force her will upon her charge. Instead she turned sorrowful eyes upon her, and Trixie would invariably exclaim, "Oh Hettie! Don't look at me like that. If it means so much to you, I'll do as you wish!" For, as has already been remarked, she was at heart a good girl.

As a result, Hester no longer felt the dread of imminent dismissal and was able to demonstrate her true value. For she was an able teacher. Though Trixie was far from bookish, Hester Wood inculcated in her the fundamentals of education. Trixie knew how to point to the important features of the globe, learned the glorious history of her homeland and memorized the names and dates of its monarchs. Greek was a closed book to her, but she learned enough Latin to understand the most popular quotations and their origins. Her understanding of French was slightly better, and she read Shakespeare, or at least those plays that were suitable for a young lady. She could compose a charming letter and write in a fine hand. If this education was not profound, it was suitable for a girl in her situation.

And quite a situation it was. As she grew in stature and a degree of wisdom, Miss Trixie Shelby discovered that she was, in fact, the Lady Beatrix. She was possessed of a substantial fortune and was expected to take an important place in society. Hester Wood had been on the outer fringes of society all her life and had a good idea of the essential qualities required of a young lady who would be at the center of it. Beatrix would one day marry a man of her own rank and become an ornament to his name. Therefore, when her charge was inclined to neglect her lessons in favor of a far from improving novel, she would sorrowfully remind her that, uninteresting though they were, it behoved her to become proficient in those arts suited to a titled lady.

She was not expected to demonstrate real expertise, of course! Heaven forbid that a lady should appear more intelligent than her husband! But as a consequence of her training, Trixie could play a nice tune on the pianoforte, so long as it did not have too many notes, sing quite delightfully, so long as the tune were not too high or low, paint a watercolor so long as a strict likeness to the original were not absolutely required, and speak French so long as a pretty accent were considered more important than absolute accuracy. Her one area of real talent was dancing. Dancing masters taught her all the steps, but it was thanks to her own aptitude that she could execute them gracefully without once looking at her feet.

Lady Beatrix's surprising attribute was a real ability in household management. As she grew older, her uncle was happy to surrender his affairs to her. She ran his life efficiently and the servants were more likely to ask her when they had any questions than to go to him. As a result, his days were ordered and peaceful. Uncle Leonard was proud of his niece and thought her very clever. As he often said to his cronies, he had all the advantages of having a delightful woman to order his life without any of the fuss and bother of marriage.

In fact, Trixie had often wondered why he had not married. She asked her godmother, Lady March, who had known him for years, why this was.

"On the face of it," she said, "he would seem a good catch. His disposition is amiable, his fortune is respectable, and he still looks quite young. He's tall and slim enough to wear those tight pantaloons and cut-away waistcoats Corny and his set wear."

"Well, my dear," replied the older lady, "the *on-dit* is that in his youth he suffered a disappointment from which he never recovered. I can remember nothing like that myself and I'm inclined to doubt the truth of it, but I have to admit it's been a useful fiction in keeping ambitious mamas from attempting to foist their daughters upon him. If you ask me," she concluded, "he likes his bachelor existence."

"Hmm," mused Beatrix. "I think he needs a good woman. I can't look after him the rest of his life and I don't know how he'll go along when I'm not here to make sure his tea has exactly the right amount of sugar, and his collars are ironed just so."

"Don't you believe it, Trixie," rejoined Lady March. "Men can always find a female to cater to their needs. He'll hire an efficient housekeeper and after a month he won't know you've gone. Don't let such considerations stand in the way of your making a good match."

Chapter Three

The long-standing tradition of the marriage mart began, of course, with the presentation of the young ladies at Court. When the time approached for Beatrix to undergo this rite of passage, her aunt the Countess found herself once more prostrated with fatigue, declaring her health would not permit her to take it on.

Trixie was in no way alarmed. Knowing her aunt's disposition and suspecting that something of the sort would happen, she had begun a full twelve months before her seventeenth birthday to mention to Uncle Leonard that her godmother would be the perfect person to bring her out.

So fixed did this idea become in Uncle Leonard's mind that when he talked of the upcoming event with Lady March, he was already considering it a *fait accompli*. Not wanting to disappoint her old friend, and being genuinely fond of Trixie, Lady March just went along with it, accompanying her to purchase the necessary gowns and holding a ball in her honor.

Trixie was not exactly beautiful but she was possessed of an enormous amount of vivacity and charm. She was full of fun and her nut brown eyes danced with pleasure, especially when the old tabbies who stood around the dance floor raised their brows at her antics. She flirted outrageously, often dressed with a distinct lack of decorum, and simply ignored anyone who criticized her. She had an excellent figure and danced like an angel. All this made her a great success that Season.

Her supporters declared her *delightfully unconventional.* Of course, had she not been heiress to twenty-five thousand a year, the description might have been *dreadfully fast.* The mamas of sons who, in vulgar parlance, needed to marry money, were of course inclined to favor the first epithets, while the mamas of daughters put into the shade by Trixie's liveliness naturally favored the second.

She received several offers from young gentlemen, and one from an older man, who saw in her a delightful companion for his declining years. She was even distinguished by an offer from the heir to the Duke of Gloucester, which was looking very high indeed. But she refused him and the others with a charm that robbed the refusal of any unpleasantness. In fact, they were all just as keen to be her friend afterwards as they had been to be her husband before.

The truth was, Lady Beatrix had never felt the least pang of love for any of them and was far from ready for marriage. She told herself it was because she was still thinking of her uncle. In spite of Lady March's assurances, she really couldn't imagine what he would do if she were to leave him. In her view, he was the person in all of London the least able to manage his affairs. And though he was the sweetest man alive, he disliked change.

She was determined to find Uncle Leonard a managing wife who would nevertheless be prepared to allow him to continue as he was. Only then could she think of removing to her own establishment, to live with that vague individual she supposed would be her husband, though no one she had yet met could remotely fill that role. Hetty, now an old lady, would of course go with her.

The Season had drawn almost to a close before the Baroness von Schwerin appeared on the scene, but this new arrival had distinct possibilities as a wife for Uncle Leonard. She was well-bred and handsome. To judge from the rigid behavior of her daughter, she would also appear to be firm. *Perfect*, she thought again.

Not a little of Trixie's success during the Season was due to a lucky accident when she was presented at Court, where she had made more of an impression than anyone could have imagined. It cannot be said she was looking her best. The white lace gown and lofty plumes could not be said to flatter her, any more than they did the majority of the other debutantes waiting in shaking anticipation for a nod from Her Majesty. Clad in this unbecoming ensemble, Trixie made her curtsey to Queen Charlotte. The queen herself was not known for her beauty. Looking up at her from her deep curtsey, Beatrix found her positively plain. She immediately lost any slight anxiety she might have felt on the occasion and favored Her Royal Highness with a friendly smile. Surprised, Queen Charlotte smiled back.

After the presentations were over, the Prince Regent, who enjoyed the event as an opportunity to ogle all the pretty girls, asked his mother what she had been smiling at.

"One of the gels smiled at me," she replied. "They usually just stare at their feet. Looked a lively gel, too. Wish I had taken note of her name. I don't usually bother. There are too many of them, year after year. That tallish one over there with Lady March." She pointed with her fan. "Brown hair."

The Regent raised his glass and stared shamelessly at Trixie who was laughing unrestrainedly at something her godmother had said. "By Jove," he said, "A bit saucy, by the looks of it. Must be, if she smiled at you like that. I must discover her name."

Chapter Four

So it was that at Almack's a week or so later, Trixie found herself being presented to the Regent himself, at his request.

"The Queen was much taken with you, my dear Lady Beatrix," he exaggerated shamelessly. "Asked me to see how you were comin' along. I shall be happy to report you are in full bloom."

Saying this, he stared openly at her bosom, for she was wearing a gown cut a trifle too low for a young lady of her age. It had not been like that originally, when Lady March went with her to buy it. But Trixie had removed the lace trim around the décolleté. It was not all she had done. At her first presentation at Almack's she had worn a pretty pink gown with a decorous neckline, entirely suitable for a maiden. But having observed the way some of the high fliers presented themselves, today she had not only removed the lace at the bosom but also dampened the petticoat under her figured muslin dress so it clung to her shapely form.

Her poor governess had nearly fainted at the sight of it. Telling her not to be silly, Trixie enveloped herself in her velvet evening cloak so that neither her uncle nor Lady March saw the scandalous effect until the moment of her presentation to the Prince. Now, having ogled her breast and run his expert eye over the rest of her, the Regent scrawled his name on her dance card before leaving for one of the card rooms.

Trixie was not surprised at the Prince's reaction. She knew his reputation. She saw no reason to conceal her charms and was confident of her ability to deal with him. She had for years been hostess at her uncle's exclusively male dinner parties. though she always left them and went to bed when the port was brought in. She was accustomed to them calling her a saucy puss and occasionally one of them, emboldened by several glasses of Leonard's excellent spirits, would try to kiss her. Though he would have been horrified to know it, she regarded the Regent in the same light: as a foolish old gentleman.

It was otherwise with Lady March, on whom her god-daughter's appearance and the Prince's reaction to it came as a profound shock.

"Good heavens!" she exclaimed. "What has that naughty girl done now? Mark my words, she'll get a reputation for being fast, and no one will offer for her. And God forbid the Regent should take a shine to her. He will ruin any other chances she might have. Not to mention the Patronesses who may decide she is *persona non grata* when they see how she appears."

"Nonsense!" responded Uncle Leonard, who had an occasional flash of perspicacity, and would brook no criticism of his beloved niece, "I've yet to hear the Prince chases after girls of seventeen, and no woman with twenty-five thousand a year, especially if she is as charming as Trixie, can ever have such a reputation that no one will offer for her. As for the Patronesses, pooh! They are all good friends of mine. They would never exclude her!"

"If they refused entrance to Almack's to the Duke of Wellington based only on the fact he wasn't wearing the required breeches," retorted his friend, "who knows what they will do?"

In the event, Uncle Leonard was proven right. When the Regent returned to claim his waltz, which had only recently been permitted at that august establishment, Trixie asked him solicitously if he might not prefer to sit and chat, the dance being perhaps a little too energetic for a gentleman of his years.

"'Pon my soul," he answered, "whatever do you mean? I can dance all night and feel none the worse for it."

"Forgive me, Your Royal Highness," replied Trixie, at her most demure. "I mean no disrespect. It's just that my uncle finds it a little much, and I believe you are of an age. Though, of course, you appear much younger," she added, mendaciously.

"And who is your uncle?" demanded the Prince, inclined to be miffed.

"Leonard Shelby. Over there, Your Royal Highness." Trixie indicated her uncle with her fan.

It has already been noted that Uncle Leonard was a well preserved, good-looking man, in fact much better-looking than the Regent, whose corpulence was now only held in check by severe corseting. So hearing himself described as appearing much younger went a long way to restoring the Prince's good humor.

"Ah, yes, I see," he said with satisfaction. "Well, I'm sure I can do better than that old fellow!"

He took Trixie's hand and led her onto the dance floor, where he proceeded to whirl her around in the most extravagant fashion, determined to prove he was more of a man than Uncle Leonard. The result was he did exhaust himself and at the end was barely able to conduct her back to her seat before collapsing in one himself.

He never again asked her to dance, but always inclined his head graciously in her direction and spoke of her as a charming gel. This meant that Trixie's star remained in the ascendant. She was not reproved by the Patronesses, nor had she any shortage of suitors.

Now, looking back at her success in the matter of her coming-out, and established at the center of the younger set of the *ton*, Trixie was preparing a campaign to marry her uncle off to the Baroness. She had absolute confidence in her ability to arrange this, and was already planning what she might wear. She rather fancied jonquil.

Chapter Five

"Uncle," said Trixie the morning after meeting the Baroness and Margarethe, "I hope you are not engaged later this afternoon, for I have undertaken that you and I should drive out in the park with a new friend of mine and her mother. They are just arrived in London and have no carriage of their own."

"Capital, my dear!" replied her uncle. "We can take my new barouche. I bought it just last week because I fear my curricle is becoming too difficult to access for ladies past their first youth."

He did not say that he was lately finding it a little difficult himself. It was a good excuse for using the new and splendid vehicle he was looking forward to showing off.

"I am hoping my bays will adapt to it. I should be loath to replace them, for a better matched team I am never likely to find again. Lord Worth once offered me an immense price for them. But that was when he was engaged on a race to Brighton with the Regent. He lost, of course. He would have won with my bays!"

It will be gathered from this response that Uncle Leonard was a fine judge of horseflesh. In his day he had been a notable whip and still kept a first class stable. He had been member of the Four Horse Club almost since its inception and still enjoyed their twice monthly meetings.

The Club was not much more than an excuse to drive a four-in-hand to Salt Hill for lunch and dinner wearing the outlandish gear demanded of members This required an ankle-length drab coat decorated with large mother-of-pearl buttons and three tiers of pockets; a blue waistcoat with inch-wide yellow stripes; knee-length breeches with strings and rosettes made of plush; and a hat that was at least three and a half inches deep in the crown. At the outset, only bay horses were permitted, but when Sir Henry Peyton showed up with a set of good-looking roans, that rule was dropped.

That afternoon saw the famed bays tossing their heads a little restively in front of the family townhouse where the Baroness and Margarethe were residing. A groom held them while Uncle Leonard helped the ladies into the barouche. It was a sumptuous, roomy affair in black lacquer with a gold interior and facing retractable hoods. It was a fine afternoon, so the hoods were both down. Everyone would be able to obtain an unimpeded view of the whole party. Trixie wanted the *ton* to get to know the von Schwerin ladies and, in particular, she wanted her uncle to get to know the Baroness. Her job would be to keep Margarethe busy introducing her to all her acquaintances. The Baroness and her uncle would thus be thrown together.

Accordingly, when her uncle handed the ladies into the barouche, she contrived to seat Margarethe next to herself and the Baroness opposite. Leonard was therefore obliged to take the other place, and found himself next to the handsome older woman.

Both ladies were expensively and modishly dressed, although as Trixie had remarked before, not in the London style. The Baroness wore a dark purple velvet cloak trimmed with black fur and done up tightly to the throat. Together with a close-fitting matching purple velvet hat and small veil, this perfectly set off her silver-gold hair which was elegantly dressed into the nape of her neck. Margarethe wore a navy blue pelisse of a somewhat military style, the stand-up collar and deep cuffs trimmed in gold braid. She, too, wore a close-fitting bonnet matching her coat. The short brim was also trimmed in gold and turned up jauntily on one side to reveal her complicated braids. It was a nice foil to her fair prettiness.

The Baroness's eyes had widened when she saw Trixie's bonnet, which was as dashing as theirs were restrained. It was an outrageous creation with an enormous poke and scarlet ribbons. It was, admittedly, a little much, but Trixie wanted to attract as much attention as possible. Besides, she liked it.

Her ploy worked. Rather little intimate conversation was to be had as the barouche was stopped at every moment by other parties taking the six o'clock air. The young gentlemen who slowed their horses to walk next to them were entranced by the contrast between Margarethe's blue-eyed flaxen prettiness and Trixie's darker curls, nut-brown eyes and fluttering scarlet ribbons.

One of their admirers was Arno Witherspoon, a slim young man with a ready smile. He rode up to their side and tipped his hat to Trixie.

"Goddesses are descended amongst us!" he declared. "We are blessed by the fair gold of Damia and the berries and chestnut of Persephone. We should bow in homage!"

He swept his hat dramatically off his head and bowed low over his horse's neck.

"Don't be silly, Arno!" responded Trixie. "You are putting my friend Margarethe von Schwerin to the blush. She is not as used to your extravagances as I am!" And turning to Margarethe, she said, "This is Arno Witherspoon, who is no doubt trying to show us he has been studying the classics after visiting the famous Marbles. I recommend you pay him no attention whatsoever."

"But I should so much like to hear about them," said Margarethe in her quiet way. "Mother and I are to visit them tomorrow with your friend Cornelius and his Mama. Perhaps Mr. Witherspoon will tell me what I should most look for."

"Did you really visit them, Arno?" asked Trixie. Receiving an affirmative, she said, "Then you'd better go around and tell Margarethe all about it. I'd be amazed if Corny will be able to. If I know him, he's more likely to tell her about the latest sensation at the races than about a collection of statues. His Mama must have prevailed upon him to go."

"Oh, no," replied her friend. "He told me he was looking forward to it."

As Arno did what he was told, and walked his horse around to Margarethe, Trixie whispered, "Arno is a dear. His mother died a year or so ago and he moved back in with his father, who was dreadfully lonely, poor thing. I see him occasionally at my uncle's get-togethers."

As they rode home, Trixie was delighted. She was sure if Corny was looking forward to a bunch of dusty old Marbles it was not because they attracted him. He must be falling in love.

Chapter Six

Not one to let the grass grow under her feet, Trixie decided the next move was a soirée with all young people, and only the Baroness to act as chaperone with her uncle. They would inevitably be drawn together. Accordingly, she said to her uncle a few days later, "I think we should have a dinner party. Only ten or twelve guests. Not so large that one may not talk to everyone at the table."

"A dinner party?" Her uncle looked up from a *sang de boeuf* vase he had just acquired. He was a collector of this dark red Chinese porcelain from the Kangxi period. "Just look at this," he said admiringly. "How the glaze has pooled in the lower part of the vessel and made it an even darker color. It's glorious."

"Yes, uncle," responded Trixie. "it is glorious. As glorious as the other twenty pieces you have in your étagère." She kissed him on the cheek. "But what about my dinner party?"

He withdrew his eyes unwillingly from the porcelain. "If you wish to have a dinner party, my dear, of course you may. I ask only that you do it before my sister-in-law the Countess arrives. You know she usually comes to London at this time of the year for a new wardrobe. The last time she came, she insisted on being carried everywhere, claiming exhaustion. All I can say is, in the end the footmen were more exhausted than she. And let us hope she doesn't bring her offspring. The girl Mariah must have driven you to distraction, following you everywhere and hanging on your arm. That boy of hers, Chauncey, mooned around like a calfling, too."

His niece giggled. "I know. Wasn't my aunt ridiculous? I suppose she thinks it makes her interesting to be constantly ailing. All it does is make her a dead bore. But Mariah will have outgrown those childish affections by now. She must be quite the young lady. And let us hope Chauncey has found something to occupy himself more than Lord Byron's poetry."

Any other guardian would have frowned at this uncharitable description of her aunt, but Leonard was used to Trixie's outspokenness. But her governess was there, carefully dusting Leonard's collection. She was the only one he trusted to do it. She tut-tutted at Trixie.

"Beatrix, my dear," she said gently. "I wish you would not talk of your aunt in such a way. You cannot know what she suffers. You are blessed with excellent health. She is not so lucky, and if her pains at times make her a little demanding, it is not to be wondered at. Last time she was here, I found her very kind and her conversation interesting. She was able to tell me a great deal about the function of the liver."

"Oh Hettie!" replied her former student fondly, "it's only because you have the patience of a saint! You sat for hours listening to her describe her symptoms. I imagine there is nothing about her liver, or any other organ, you don't know. Bless you! I don't know what we would have done without you! Anyway," she continued, turning to her uncle, "Have no fear. For my party, I intend to invite only young people who can perambulate on their own two legs and don't even know they have a liver. And the

Baroness von Schwerin will keep you company. You like her, don't you?"

"Very much. She is a perfect lady. She will ensure we don't become too rowdy."

"You see, Hettie," said Trixie, satisfied that her plan to bring her uncle and the Baroness together was proceeding nicely, "you may safely leave us with the Baroness. Do not feel you have to chaperone us. I know you would rather dine quietly in your room."

This was true. Miss Wood was by now an old lady and the prospect of a dinner party was not at all to her liking, particularly if it was liable to be rowdy. It was becoming hard for her to follow too many conversations at once.

"You notice I don't assume my dear uncle will be a sufficient chaperone," continued Trixie, smiling at him. "You are so youthful, uncle, you will probably be the rowdiest of us all!"

Her uncle chuckled in appreciation and pinched her cheek. "With you amongst us, how can we be anything but lively?"

Ignoring this, but wanting to keep the focus of the conversation on Margarethe's mother, Trixie replied, "The Baroness certainly is a most lovely lady, but one knows so little about her. Corny told me a little, but with him, one can never be sure it's not just gossip. Did she tell you anything about how they come to be here during our ride the other day? Margarethe and I were so besieged I had no chance to ask her anything of that nature."

"Yes. It's a tangled story. They come from the Duchy of Mecklenburg-Schwerin, in the northern part of Germany. The Baroness, who is English, met her German husband in London, oh, it must be close to thirty years ago, when he was here on a diplomatic mission. On the death of his father they moved to the Duchy to take up his inheritance. After that upstart Bonaparte started his rampage through Europe, the place seems to have had a very checkered history, the army fighting first on the side of the French, and then for the allies of Britain. Sadly, the Baron was killed in one of the engagements. Then the Baroness's father died. He was here in England, of course, but things were so bad on the Continent, she could not come home until now. He had a large unentailed estate in Wiltshire he left to her son, who is there now, sorting things out. He inherits the German title and property as well, of course."

Hettie shook her head in sympathy with the Baroness and her family. "How dreadful!" she said. "We must thank God we live here in this peaceful land."

"It does make our life here seem very tame," agreed Trixie. She pondered for a moment. "Margarethe is a very private person, it seems. She did mention she had a brother, but she didn't say anything about all that. I wonder what he's like. I do hope he'll come to London. I wonder if he's very strict and Teutonic."

She walked around stiff-legged, saluting all the furniture in a ramrod way, ending with the *sang de boeuf* vase, saying in an exaggeratedly too-perfect English, "Good afternoon, Sir Sang de Boeuf. I hope you do not find the pooling of your glaze too uncomfortable in your nether regions."

Miss Wood frowned at this levity, but Uncle Leonard laughed and slapped his knee.

"You are a naughty puss, and no mistake! But you shouldn't make fun of this Baron. He has apparently had a hard time of it. Besides, I daresay he's a very a good-looking man if his mother and sister are anything to go by. When he finally gets to London, you may fall in love with him and end up with him as your husband."

"Nothing is more unlikely," said Trixie gaily. "Anyway, any husband of mine had better be used to being made fun of. I want someone with a sense of humor."

"But you must respect him, for all that," replied her governess. "Domestic felicity cannot prevail if a wife doesn't respect her husband."

"If he earns my respect, I shall," said Trixie. "I do not honor people merely because they have rank or money."

Invitations to the dinner party were sent out and because Trixie had investigated the availability of the guests beforehand, were all accepted. It was to be ten days hence. Nothing had been heard from the exhausted Countess, so they were safe.

In the meantime, Trixie again mentioned casually to her uncle how unfortunate it was that the Baroness had no carriage of her own, but so enjoyed a ride. Margarethe had explained that neither of them was a judge of horses or knew anything about the modern carriages available in London. They would have to wait for her brother to choose them. It was a pity he had been away longer than any of them had expected.

Trixie knew her hints would not fall on deaf ears, and it was not long before the Baroness and her daughter were invited for another ride, and Uncle Leonard had put himself at the Baroness's disposal in the matter of carriages and horses.

By the time the evening of the dinner came around, the two families were on the best of terms. They had been to tea more than once, Trixie had discovered that Margarethe was an accomplished pianist, and the Baroness and her daughter could be seen almost every day being sedately driven in an elegant barouche with a pair of perfectly matched chestnuts.

The dinner party was an unqualified success from all points of view. Told that a number of young people would be at table, the cook wisely decided on a menu that was copious and simple.

Fillets of cod with an oyster sauce and a fricassé of mushrooms were removed with a fine loin of beef, and a ragout of veal was presented with roasted parsnips, leek tartlets, and green peas. The young ladies were especially pleased with the selection of jellies, creams and spun sugar confections that ended the meal.

Since Trixie was accustomed to acting as hostess for her uncle, as a matter of course she placed him at one end of the table and herself at the other. She seated the Baroness on his right and a pretty debutante on his left. She knew he would be well satisfied with both. The ingénue would make him feel young, and she was hoping the older one was by now becoming more than a friend.

She had placed her friend Corny on her own right with Margarethe next to him, and one of her rejected suitors on her left. She turned resolutely to him, knowing that Corny would be obliged by convention to engage Margarethe on his other side. She was pleased to overhear snatches of conversation about the Elgin Marbles.

The meal was accompanied by an excellent selection of wines from her uncle's cellar, and once the glasses had been refilled, with no disapproving mamas to supervise the company, it became very lively. Conversation became general amongst the younger set, leaving Uncle Leonard and the Baroness to each other. Trixie saw this and congratulated herself.

"It is so kind of you to invite me with my daughter," the Baroness was saying. "I don't know that I have ever been at a dinner with so many young people! We used to live in a somewhat remote spot and Margarethe has had little opportunity to meet people of her own age and, er… situation."

"Trixie suggested it," said Leonard. "She is the dearest girl. She thinks of nothing but my happiness and the happiness of those around her."

"She has no beau, if I may ask so personal a question?"

"She has had several offers, including one from a Duke, though he was a very pallid youth and it would never have been a good match. Even the Prince Regent has distinguished her, but no, so far no one has been lucky enough to engage her heart."

"It will take a man of unusual character to be the right husband for her, I think," responded the Baroness. "She is accustomed to great freedom and running things as she wants. Not every man would be able to handle that."

"He'd just have to let her have her head, as I do," said Leonard. "We have always been perfectly happy."

If the Baroness had doubts that many gentlemen would be so complaisant, she kept her own counsel.

At length, Lady Beatrix rose, signaling it was time for the ladies to leave the gentlemen to their port. The gentlemen, who stood when the ladies left, grouped themselves at their host's end of the table and were gratified beyond measure when they were treated to a bottle of Uncle Leonard's vintage 1797 port.

The ladies, having refreshed themselves in the bedchambers provided for their use, settled in the salon. There was general gossip until Trixie decided it was time for Margarethe to demonstrate her excellence on the pianoforte. When the gentlemen came in, she would be discovered at the instrument and would present so pretty a picture, Corny would fall even deeper in love. She begged her friend to play.

"I implore you, Margarethe! Otherwise uncle will make me play, and I'm not nearly as good as you are. I tell you what, if you play something nice first, then we can do a couple of songs together."

The Baroness overheard her and knew perfectly well her uncle would make her do nothing she did not want. But she was glad Trixie was persuading Margarethe to show her talents a little; her daughter would never put herself forward.

A Mozart Sonata was already lying on the pianoforte, not by chance, it must be said, and Margarethe obediently began to play it. She played well, with a delicate touch and an obvious love of the music, so it was not surprising that when the gentlemen came in they fell silent and sat quietly to listen. When the piece came to an end, there were genuine cries of *encore,* but, as promised, Trixie went over to Margarethe, sorted through a pile of songs that also just happened to be available, and chose two or three. She began with the popular *Bonny Light Horseman*, with the refrain:

Broken-hearted I'll wander,
Broken-hearted I'll wander,
My bonny light horseman that was slain in the wars.

It was a very pretty song and Trixie liked it, but as she sang she realized that, talking as it did about a Hussar slain in the Napoleonic Wars, it could hardly appeal to the Baroness and Margarethe. She ended it quickly and moved on to the simple folksongs of the lad and his maid variety. The first was *As I Walked Through The Meadow*, with a message that made some of the young gentlemen hoot:

Said I: Pretty maiden, shall I go with you,
To the meadows to gather some may?
O no, sir, she said, I would rather refuse,
For I fear you would lead me astray.

Lastly she began *Billy Boy*, with Billy telling his mother that the girl he has chosen:

Is as fit to be my wife as a fork is to a knife,
But she's too young to be taken from her mother

Margarethe began to sing as soon as she saw how these songs went, and they were joined by most of the young men, including Cornelius and Arno, who loudly sang the innumerable verses, some of them very silly indeed.

After that, the guests began to propose their favorites, which Margarethe picked up very quickly and accompanied without sheet music. As these things happen, the offering became more and more foolish, till they were all singing nursery rhymes and other nonsense. It was loud and not very tuneful.

The music, if such it could be called by that time, ended when the butler brought in the tea tray. This was accompanied by small almond cakes, which the company fell on as if it had not eaten a copious meal a mere two hours before. Groups sat around for a while chatting and laughing, but everyone knew this signaled the end of the evening.

The Baroness and her daughter were the first to leave, fully aware that as the guests of honor no one could leave before them.

"I've never had such an agreeable evening in my life," said Margarethe, her face glowing.

"It would not have been nearly as agreeable without you," replied Trixie, and meant it. "You are so clever on the piano. Even our silly songs sounded good!"

"I didn't know any of these silly songs, as you call them, but they are such fun! I am familiar with some of our *lieder* in German, but they are always very serious."

"Thank you, my dear," said the Baroness, pressing Trixie's hand. "I see what your uncle means when he says no one can be unhappy around you. It's very good for Margarethe. I'm afraid we haven't had many opportunities for laughing in the last months."

Uncle Leonard accompanied the ladies into the hall, while Trixie went into the drawing room to encourage the others to depart.

"Off you go," she said, without preamble. "Time to go home."

As the others began to drift out into the hall where the butler handed them their cloaks, coats, canes and hats, Trixie stopped Cornelius.

"Margarethe is so clever, don't you think, besides being pretty?"

"She certainly is," said Cornelius, "quite exceptional."

Trixie smiled. Things were progressing nicely.

Chapter Seven

Lukas von Schwerin was bone-tired as he went up the front steps of Chorley House. It was where he had spent most of his happy youth. His mother had wanted her son to be educated in her homeland, and her husband, the Baron, a confirmed anglophile, had not objected. He had always loved his wife's country. So Lukas had come to England when he was ten and had received the classic education of an English gentleman. He had spent most of his holidays in this house with his grandparents.

This calm existence had come to an abrupt end when, just as he completed his studies at Oxford, Bonaparte had invaded his homeland. As his mother had told Uncle Leonard, it was a dreadful time. She had sent urgent letters encouraging her son to stay where he was, but for him, it was unthinkable that he should abandon his family. He crossed the Channel as soon as he could and swapped his English clothes with the first person he saw of his size, thinking, rightly, that a European gentleman would be less remarkable than an obviously English one. He made the precarious trip across Europe posing as a German teacher returning home. He arrived in time to be forced, along with his father, into the German contingent of the Grande Armée of the

French Empire. Bonaparte had decided to bring the Russians to heel.

The ill-fated campaign began in June under a driving rain followed by scorching sun that dried the roads into ruts and broke the horses' legs. The old Baron and his son were put in charge of one of the units responsible for the provisioning requirements for the huge army. They tried to do this honestly by paying farmers for the things they needed, but as time went on and food became scarcer they were aware that pillaging became rampant.

They struggled towards Moscow as the weather grew colder, the forward lines following but rarely meeting the enemy who withdrew further and further into the country. The French army units were also further and further from their supply lines. Men were starving. The soldiers' hard biscuits were infested with weevils. Horses were slaughtered for meat, seasoned with the gunpowder they were unable to use on an enemy that wouldn't stand and fight. Vegetables were unobtainable and even the vinegar the men drank to ward off scurvy ran out.

By October they knew that Bonaparte had misjudged both the conditions and Russian determination. Finally, in November, they met soldiers coming back towards them with the news that rather than let it fall to the enemy, the Russians had burned Moscow. The exhausted French army, unable to obtain essential re-provisioning, was forced to simply turn back.

With Bonaparte making all haste back to France, Grand Duke Frederick Francis of Mecklenburg-Schwerin was the first of the German rulers to abandon him. Having made their difficult way back home, Lukas and his father were sent with their countrymen to join Britain and her allies against the French. The Baron died in a skirmish on the side of the British a few months later, shot from his horse. His son held him as he died, his blood on his hands.

Lukas was devastated; he had not spent much of his youth with his father, but the months with him in the army of the French Empire had given them the closeness of a lifetime together. Only one thing consoled him: he was glad that if his father had to meet his end, he had done so on the side of his long-time friends and not the hated enemy.

With Bonaparte on the run, the Grand Duke gave Lukas a dispensation to return home to his mother and sister. It was a time of grief upon grief. His beloved grandmother had died while he was in Russia and he longed to console his grandfather, but the trip back to England was still perilous, and his family needed him.

Then the deposed French Emperor, exiled too close to home on the Italian island of Elba, escaped and marched north to meet the combined forces of Europe. The scattered French army attached itself to him as he went. Lukas served again with the German coalition against the French and was distinguished at the siege of Montmédy, though he never saw action at the Battle of Waterloo, which finally brought the era of Bonaparte to a close. By the winter of 1815 he was home once again, thin, exhausted and suffering from nightmares.

Not two months later, they received news of the death of his grandfather. His mother was bereft. She had not seen either of her parents for years before they died. Lukas was both his father's and his maternal grandfather's heir, and had to hold up the family in face of this third great loss. Outwardly, he remained stalwart as he tried to piece their lives back together. But inwardly he suffered.

He was more English than German. He felt a stranger there in the Duchy and soon mistrusted the motivation of the Grand Duke. The man was a reactionary and, far from advancing the light of democracy that had begun to burn in Europe, he would extinguish it entirely if he could. The Duchy was practically medieval. Lukas found himself longing for the soft green of England and the independent spirit of its people.

So when his mother, who was finding it difficult to live there without her husband, asked him to consider moving the whole family back to her homeland, she found him more than willing. He leased the estate to a neighbor, found tenants for the house, and, taking those of the servants who wished to come and a few family items they were all fond of, moved in a cavalcade of lumbering carriages across Europe.

Now here he was, standing in front of the English home that was his. Chorley House was a big old weathered stone edifice surrounded by an ancient grove of trees protecting it from the wind that seemed to blow constantly there. It stood at the center of a large sheep farm in the central plain of Wiltshire and had been in the family for generations. The wide gravel path to the front steps was no longer as clear of weeds as it had been in his youth, the flower beds were overgrown and the grass needed to be scythed. Labor had become scarce as countrymen joined Wellington's army and he knew his grandfather had not been able, in the end, to keep up with it all. Lukas rode over the whole estate, where the half-empty sheep pens looked dilapidated and more fields were fallow than cultivated.

He was determined to put Chorley Manor on the path to a solid footing before he left for London. Besides, he found that if he worked himself to a standstill he might be able to sleep for a few hours before the dreams began. The screaming of wounded men and the smell of his father's blood on his hands would wake him up, sweating and trembling.

He had already sent a note to the estate manager, a Mr. Goodwin, to be there at nine the following morning. He had never met the man and hoped he wasn't going to have to dismiss him. Goodwin had replaced old Smithers who used to let Lukas ride along when he was a boy, teaching him how to help with the lambing or snare the biggest rabbits that ran rampant over the plain.

He stepped into the wide hall. His grandmother had always kept a bowl of rose petals on the great oak trunk in there, and he waited for the elusive scent to reach his nose. But though the trunk was still there, polished and solid, the empty bowl had nothing to offer. He did smell his grandfather's pipe as he walked into the drawing room. That made him smile. He remembered his grandmother chasing her husband out of there, complaining about the nasty smelly thing. But after she was gone, the old man had evidently taken what comfort he could, where he could. Now he was gone, too.

An old dog lay in front of the fireplace, and at Lukas' step, it looked up. It was an old gun dog, sandy colored, with intelligent eyes and a smooth coat, now greying around the muzzle. Her eyes brightened as she saw Lukas, and she clambered to her feet, her long tail waving.

"Juno?" said Lukas. He remembered the young dog his grandfather had bought when he was at Eton. She must be eleven years old by now.

"Hello, old girl," he said, sitting down in his grandfather's old chair to pat the dog's head. "I'm so glad to see you! I was wondering whether anything here would be the same."

Juno licked his hand and put her grizzled muzzle on Lukas's knee.

"You're sleeping the time away instead of going out hunting, nowadays, are you old lady? I wish I could do the same." Lukas pulled gently at the dog's ears. "I feel I could sleep for a hundred years."

He dropped his hand for a moment as his mind wandered, and the dog thrust its muzzle under it, urging him to continue.

"Master Luke?" a voice sounded behind him, and he turned his head to see a lady in the black, high-throated gown and white apron of the housekeeper. She was plain and flat chested, her thin hair scraped into a bun at the back of her head.

Lukas stood up and looked at her. "It's Mollie, isn't it?" he said, smiling.

"Mrs. Truly, now," she replied. "Not that I was ever married, but now I'm housekeeper I'm called Mrs."

She had been a downstairs maid when he was a boy, always plain and not much to look at. But many's the time she had saved him puddings or cakes before he was old enough to go to the dinner parties his grandparents hosted. She would bring them up to his room with a glass of milk and tell him who was downstairs. She had a sharp tongue and wouldn't spare in her descriptions of anyone she didn't like. There was a neighborhood matron who prided herself on her family connections but was a renowned skinflint.

"And there she is, looking down her nose at us and thinking we wouldn't notice her old dress furbished up with a bit of lace. Terrible nip-cheese she is! I hear it from her Nellie, who's my bosom-bow. Wouldn't spit on a man in flames!"

Lukas would laugh with her, secure in the knowledge that as much as she was scathing of those she disliked, she was his friend.

He now took both her hands and said, "How pleased I am to see you, Mollie, er, Mrs. Truly. I began to think I would never see another familiar face."

"The master and mistress spoke of you often, and wished they could see you. But they said as how you were stuck over there with That Man! It must have been terrible, with all those foreigners. I don't know how you could stand it, Master Luke, and that's a fact. Oh, I'm so sorry, Master Luke, Baron, Sir, I mean!"

"Well, I couldn't bear it, so I'm here now, and my mother and sister are in London waiting to come here too. I suspected the place might need some work. I didn't want my mother to see her old home looking anything but its best. And yes, I suppose you must call me Baron." He stopped for a moment. "But I wish I could erase the last few years and go back to when I was still Master Luke and you were Mollie." He sighed. "But we can't turn the clock back. I must put things in order before bringing my mother and sister here. We're settling in England. I expect they'll spend part of the year here and the Season in London. They're in grandfather's townhouse at the moment."

"And welcome they'll be! How long it must be since the Baroness was here! She left before I came. Now, don't you go working too hard, Master... Baron, Sir, so tired as you look — and so tall! You must have grown a foot since I last saw you! You stay here a while, along of me, and we'll get you fixed up right as a trivet so you can go to London for your Mama and find yourself a nice wife. That's what you need, to make you comfortable."

"A wife?" he laughed ruefully. "I'm a long way from that! First things first. I must meet with the estate manager tomorrow morning. Send Robbins to me, would you? I need to talk to him about various arrangements."

"Robbins the butler, sir? I'm afraid he retired. He only waited till your grandfather passed on. You'll want to promote one of the footmen to butler, I should think, sir. William is the best choice. He's been waiting all these years and I think he'll serve you well. You don't want someone as doesn't know the place, sir, with everything else being new."

"Of course! I should have thought of that. Robbins must be an old man by now. He deserves his retirement. Send William to me, if you think that's best. I'm counting on you. You always did look after me, Mollie, I mean, Mrs. Truly!"

Juno pushed her head against Lukas's legs, tired of being ignored. He bent and patted her.

"Look at that," said the housekeeper. "She won't go to anyone in the house since the Master died. Just lays there where he always used to sit. Only comes down to the kitchens to be fed and go out once in a while. If anyone tries to touch her, she growls. Not that I think she'd hurt a soul. She's always been the gentlest animal alive. But she's grieving and wants to be left alone."

"She must remember me from when we were both young together," said Lukas.

"And she sees your grandfather in you, sir. Like we all do, and that's a fact."

Lukas smiled. "I'm happy to hear that. He was a fine man."

"Indeed he was, sir. Indeed he was." She curtsied and left.

While he was waiting for the candidate for butler, he sat, absent-mindedly pulling at Juno's ears again. A wife! He hadn't thought about that, but it was true. He was now owner of two estates, and he must make sure of an heir. Something else to worry about. He sighed again. Juno sighed too, her head on Lukas's knee, but for her it was at the joy of having someone she loved pull at her ears.

Chapter Eight

A month after the dinner party, Uncle Leonard received the communication they were dreading. He grimaced and made its contents known to his ward.

Shelby Place, the 30th of September
Dear Brother,
I intend to come to London for a month now that the hot weather is over. I cannot endure the heat, and the noise with the windows open oversets my nerves. But I am needing some new gowns, and although occasionally she needs direction there is no one like Beatrix's Céleste to make them. Chauncey and Mariah will come with me this time, but the Earl will stay at home. The estate is especially demanding at this time of the year.

"No it isn't," laughed Trixie. "The harvest must be in and there's precious little to do. He's just glad to see the back of them! And what does she mean by Céleste needing direction? That's the first I've heard of it!"

It will be good for Mariah to see a little of London society this year. She is already thinking of her coming out. I hope dear Lady Beatrix will show her how to go

*on, though perhaps without her own degree of
liveliness.*

"What cheek!" exclaimed the dear Lady Beatrix. "If Mariah is still as clinging as she was last time, a degree of her own liveliness wouldn't come amiss!"

*Chauncey has been preparing for his exams at
Oxford and the poor boy is sadly pulled. A few rides
and outings in interesting company will do him a world
of good.*

"Well, I hope he brings his own horses," said Leonard. "I'm damned if I let him ruin mine. A more cow-fisted rider I'm never likely to see!"

*I imagine the question of my bedchamber must be
troubling you, dear Brother. I am aware that Lady
Beatrix occupies the best front room, which one would
normally expect to see offered to the senior lady. But
since it is on the front of the house with the
abominable traffic at all times of the day and night, I
must declare myself satisfied with the secondary
chamber at the back. If you will have the bed moved
away from the windows and new linens put upon it,
with extra pillows for my back, it will do. New curtain
and bed hangings will also be needed. I found them
dusty last year, and you know my lungs are so
sensitive.*

"Move the bed? New linens and hangings?" cried Trixie. "Does she imagine herself Queen Elizabeth?"

*You will no doubt be amazed at the simplicity of my
requirements, dear Brother, and for my generosity in
accepting the secondary chamber. As it overlooks the
garden, I may hope for a few moments of peace,
which, as you know, is so easily disturbed. I am a*

martyr to my nerves, and never more so than when I travel.

"Then why doesn't she stay at home?" cried uncle and niece together.

We expect to be with you Monday se'ennight if I am able to complete the journey in only two days. The bumping of the roads is intolerable to me, and if my headache should happen to come on, we may have to stop more often.

Your devoted sister,

Amahlia, Countess of Westhampnet

"Two days!" cried Trixie. "It's only twenty-five miles! Oh Lord! I foresee endless trips to Céleste, ordering gowns, changing her mind, finding fault with something, taking them back... it will be a nightmare! And a silly girl and her brother who's about as interesting as a codfish! Now we are in the basket!"

"That boy is not riding my horses," mused her uncle, still in his own thoughts. "I think I might buy that showy grey Bimstead was offering last week. I know for a fact it's a slug with a mouth like a stone. Not good for my reputation, of course, but it can't be helped. At least I should be able to get it cheap."

They looked at each other in despair.

The Countess, her offspring, and an overweight pug, duly arrived in an enormous old coach with the family coat of arms emblazoned on the side. *In Omnes Potentia.* Power in Everything. A singularly inappropriate motto, given that she was in a state of prostration and had to be supported into the house, the pug yapping behind her. A second coach arrived with her maid and all the luggage, of which there was so much it took the two footmen all afternoon to carry it upstairs. That was after they had carried up the Countess herself in a chair. She was no lightweight, having spent her life exercising her limbs as little as possible and reinforcing herself with sweetmeats, which were the only thing, she said, that she could stomach.

Fortunately for her, she had found a physician who swiftly understood and prescribed precisely that regimen. She called him in so regularly he stood in hopes of an early retirement. It was only the most forcible representations of her husband that prevented her taking him to London for the month and lodging and nourishing him at her brother-in-law's expense.

"On your head be it, husband," she said petulantly. "If I should suffer an attack and be carried off without the ministrations of dear Dr. Thompson."

"Faced with such a sad but unexpected outcome, I should have to bear up as best I might," replied her life's partner, which response she was wise not to question too closely.

Luckily for the rest of the family, her ladyship kept to her bed for three days, the pug by her side, so that except for responding to her querulous demands for copies of the latest *Mode Illustrée*, chocolate macaroons and more blankets for her feet, most of which were catered to by Hettie, they were able to go about their own business.

Trixie had been right when she surmised that Mariah would have outgrown her childish clinging. She was now a bouncing fifteen year-old. She had the same type of looks as her mother as a girl, being buxom and pink cheeked, with brown curly hair, eyes to match, and a neat ankle. For the last year she had become accustomed to being admired in the neighborhood. She had heard herself described by the gentlemen as a very pretty gel and, though she was not supposed to have heard it, by the local squire as *fair set to be a delicious armful.*

Her head was in a fair way to being turned, and she was already looking forward to a triumphant coming out. She had confidently told her best friend she expected to be advantageously married before she was eighteen.

Consequently, when riding out in the park with Trixie, she brazenly ogled all the young men and quizzed her cousin on her beaux.

"None?" she said incredulously, when Trixie replied in the negative.

"None that are serious," laughed Trixie.

"But the Season is nearly over! I should be mortified to get to the end of my second Season without an offer!"

"Oh, I've had offers," replied Trixie airily, "but none that I would call husband material."

This was a new idea to the young lady, who thought all nice-looking men under thirty were husband material, provided of course, they had sufficient fortune. But her Papa would see to all that.

"How do you know? If they're husband material, I mean."

"Well, I couldn't live with someone who's boring or addicted to low sports or stays out all night playing cards."

"What are low sports?" This was something new. The girl was agog.

Trixie began to wish she hadn't introduced this topic, but then thought that, on the whole, it was best that Mariah be informed. "Things like cock fighting or boxing in cellars for money or… or…." She was on the verge of telling her what Corny had told her, about what went on in the sluices of Tothill Fields, where men of all walks of life engaged in betting on any number of disreputable activities, but decided enough was enough. "Or things like that."

Mariah looked at her with round eyes. "But how would you know?" she asked. Presumably her brother didn't have the same pastimes as Corny, or if he did (which she doubted) he didn't tell his sister about it.

"You ask them to take you riding or meet you in the park at ten in the morning. Say there's nothing you like more than the morning air. If they look at you as if you're mad and make excuses, you know they are in the habit of staying out all night, and you draw your own conclusions. The same goes for cards. You don't want to be married to a man who may lose his fortune gambling."

Now she was into it, she thought she might as well give her cousin the benefit of her experience. Not for nothing had she been hostess to her uncle's bachelor dinner parties. At least, she had always withdrawn at the end of dinner and disappeared upstairs, but she had overheard a great deal and knew what gentlemen meant when they referred to *highflyers* and *bits of muslin*. She knew that some became so involved they had to pay the women off to prevent a scandal.

"Another thing men don't want you to know is if they haunt the back stage of the opera and are, er, entertained by dancers. That's harder to learn, because, of course, they don't flaunt those women in society... usually. But if you listen to their conversations with other men, they often let things drop. The thing is, they think we're too stupid or innocent to know anything about it. I asked my friend Cornelius once if he had a bit of muslin and he blushed so red it made me laugh! He said it's not the sort of thing a lady should talk about, and anyway, men were different from women, and what if he did, it was none of my business. So that answered that question. I mean, if Corny has an opera dancer, everyone must have one. I blame the Prince Regent. He has so many mistresses he forgets their names. So I decided if I were ever thinking of marriage, I should ask my beau point blank. I shouldn't mind if he were honest about it and promised to give up all that sort of thing after we were married. I don't want to be like

Princess Caroline. Though, of course, they say she has lovers, too."

Mariah looked at her in amazement. Trixie, realizing what she had said, added quickly, "You must understand, Mariah, living in London one knows all sorts of things. There's no need to repeat to your Mama all I've told you."

"No, indeed," said her cousin. She sat back against the leather of the barouche, her head spinning. Trixie talked of the Prince Regent as if he were, well, just any other man! And Princess Caroline! Lovers! Bits of muslin! No, she certainly wouldn't repeat a word of it to her mother.

It was normal that Trixie's cousins should soon become acquainted with Margarethe von Schwerin. Both found her a charming girl. Chauncey liked her because she did not scoff at his poor horsemanship and love of poetry. Mariah liked her because she listened with every appearance of interest to her stories about parties at home and the beaux, real or imagined, who had brought her posies and little gifts wrapped in ribbon.

"It is so different from customs in my home," said Margarethe. "We are not permitted at all to meet with men unchaperoned. We could not receive any gift. Our fathers arrange our marriage. Once a man has been chosen, we may sit with him, with an older female in the room. Perhaps he may offer us a bouquet or a poem, but only once the chaperone has seen it is unexceptional. I have found it so exhilarating to see the free way men and women mingle here in London. It is not what I am at all accustomed to."

Both Mariah and Trixie exclaimed in horror at the idea of having one's husband chosen and of not being able to talk to anyone one wanted.

"I believe it used to be that way here," said Trixie, "but this is not the eighteenth century! Things are different now."

"And think how romantic it is to meet your beau in the moonlight!" cried Mariah. In fact, she had never done such a thing, since her father was almost as strict as those Margarethe had described, but she had heard stories.

"Walking in the moonlight with a gentleman?" said Margarethe, wonderingly.

"Yes. Or if your lover comes to your window in the moonlight. Like *Romeo and Juliet*," said Trixie. "Except you don't go in some silly cave and drink poison and die. You fly with him on a snow-white horse and live in a garret, until you find he's a Prince and his kingdom is restored to him."

She saw the two other girls looking at her in astonishment. "Have you never read the novels of Mrs. Radcliffe or Mr. Walpole?" Trixie had fed herself on a diet of these for as long as she could remember, for her uncle paid no attention, and poor Hettie had given up. She thought them jolly good fun.

In spite of her pretended worldliness, Mariah had no first-hand experience of these novels, as her father had strictly forbidden them in the house, so she was as ignorant as Margarethe of this type of literature. When both girls answered they had never been allowed, or in Margarethe's case, never even heard of, the thrilling works of these writers and others like them, Trixie promised to look out her old copies. It was not long before both girls were immersed in *The Castle of Otranto* and *The Mysteries of Udolpho*.

In fact, Trixie grew quite vexed with Mariah, who never seemed to want to do anything but sit in the window seat in her room and read the day away. Her natural inclination was to be as indolent as her mother, and reading gave her an excuse to indulge it, sighing extravagantly over affecting passages.

"Listen to this," she said when Trixie came upon her one day. "When Valancourt tries to get her to elope with him, it says about

Emily, *She spoke not; her cheek was cold, and her senses seemed to fail her, but she did not faint*. Is that how one feels if a man asks one to elope? I wonder if it would make me faint?"

"Well, let's hope you never find out," replied Trixie with a laugh. "I've always thought eloping must be most uncomfortable. One may take only a bandbox, so when one's gown becomes dreadfully crushed one has nothing to change into, nor any maid to help. And then one is forced to ride for hours in a cold and dirty coach, or across the saddle of a horse! How unpleasant!"

"But if one is in love, it must be so romantic!" sighed Mariah. "You wouldn't notice the miles if you were gazing into the eyes of your beloved."

"That sounds even worse! It would be most dreadfully dull! Besides, how could he see where you were both going if he was gazing into your eyes the whole time?"

"Oh Trixie! You have no romance in your soul! I can't understand why you read all these wonderful stories if they didn't move you!"

"They did move me, they made me laugh! Come on, Mariah, let's go for a walk, for heaven's sake. You've been on that seat all day!"

"No! I'm dying to see what happens!"

"But you know what's going to happen! The lovers will be united, there will be plenty of money, and the evil plotters will all perish. It's the same every time!"

"I know," cried Mariah, "but I want to see *how* it all works out. It's fascinating! How did Mrs. Radcliffe think it all up?"

"Oh, these novelists, they just think of the most unlikely thing and make it happen. Anyone could do it, really."

But Mariah was already back in her book and didn't hear her.

Chapter Nine

It was probably as well that after three days their discussions came to an end because the Countess condescended to being carried downstairs and taken out for gentle drives with them. It took Trixie pulling in front and Mariah pushing from behind to get her up the steps of the barouche, but her ladyship enjoyed it as much as she was capable of enjoying anything. To be sure, the sun was too hot and she needed a parasol, or the wind too sharp and she needed another shawl, but on the whole, with pug warm on her lap, she was relatively content. Mariah still ogled the young men, but did it now with a degree of circumspection that told Trixie she'd learned something.

The following week they made the first trip to Céleste, the expensive modiste who had enjoyed Lady Beatrix's custom since she came out. She was a small, darting woman who had left Paris after the death of Robespierre. Her husband was a *sans-culottes*, whose revolutionary ideas became more extreme the more he drank. Luckily he was usually too drunk to actually do anything, so he had not so far been arrested, but Céleste saw the tide was turning against the extremists and decided to come to London while she could.

An expert needlewoman, she had always been the money earner in the family, but with anyone who looked like a noblewoman having been sent to Madame La Guillotine, and those who escaped not daring to spend their money on finery, her income had dropped. She thought she would do better in London.

She had told her husband she would send for him when she was settled, but she had met up with another émigrée like herself who was a milliner, and they had thrown in their lot together. Her husband had been forgotten.

From the start they had decided their gowns and bonnets would be very exclusive and very expensive. They began by offering their services free of charge to three or four aristocratic ladies each of whom was assured she was the only one receiving this benefit. The modistes claimed the others had paid extraordinary sums for what they were wearing. Naturally, word of these sums got out, and not one of the ladies refuted the gossip. It increased their stature no end for others to know (or think they knew) how much they had paid for their gowns.

Their products were genuinely very fine and in the latest mode, but it was the price that made them so desirable, for who does not want to be seen wearing what others cannot afford? Their fame soon spread and new customers were not surprised when the sums they were charged were eye-watering. And then, to ensure their reputation for exclusivity, they routinely turned customers away.

This brilliant plan quite soon made them better off than either of them had ever been. They found a large house just on the edge of fashionable London, where they established *Céleste et Marie: Modes Parisiennes*. They lived in a comfortable apartment in the back, cooked themselves delicious little meals and planned an eventual retirement in the country. They would grow vegetables and raise chickens. And perhaps a pig.

Lady Beatrix was a favorite with Céleste and Marie. She had a lovely figure, was prepared to try any extravagant novelty, and never even looked at a bill. They were all sent to Uncle Leonard, who in turn gave them to their man of business without glancing at them. If the man of business was the one whose eyes watered, he never said anything. Lady Beatrix's fortune made thrift unnecessary.

The Countess was not a favorite with them. They only tolerated her because of Trixie. In fact, Céleste had intimated to Lady Beatrix last time that "'Er Ladysheep is too, 'ow you say, too fussee. She make much work for nuzzing. Ze gown is *parfait*. We are vairy beezy and 'ave not time for zeeze *balivernes*." By which Trixie understood that her aunt's nonsense might lead to Céleste's refusing to continue with her. She told her aunt this, as delicately as she could, But her ladyship pooh-poohed it.

But when, after taking receipt of the first gown, she found some trifling problem with it and carried it back, Céleste pronounced herself too busy to make any changes and suggested she might like to go to… and here she named another dressmaker. The Countess immediately clutched her bosom in anguish.

But not all the fainting, palpitations, and signs of imminent fatal collapse she was capable of changed the modiste's polite but firm demeanor. She was forced to take the offending garment back home unchanged. She retreated to her bed for two days. But it made no difference. She had to accept that gown and any other Céleste made for her as they were, or never go to the modiste again. Céleste won.

The Countess took uncomplaining receipt of a second gown, and when her appearance was much applauded, she told herself and her intimates that she had been right to point out the minor error in the first, for Céleste had obviously not repeated it. She had been in the right, after all. And no one said anything when, after a couple of weeks, her ladyship wore the unaltered first gown to similar universal applause. *Evidently*, she told herself, *the fault is only noticeable to anyone with such a highly discerning eye as myself.*

It is not to be supposed that Mariah stood idly by while these expensive confections were made for her mother. She persuaded her fond Mama to let her have one too. When it came, even the Countess had to admit that, as mistaken as she still declared Céleste to have been in the matter of her first garment, her taste in what she made for her daughter was impeccable. The gown was in a soft apple-green silk, which suited Mariah's complexion to perfection. It was cut sufficiently low to display her ample charms, but not so low as to be unbecomingly bold. Indeed, she had wanted it lower. Her mother might have given in, but Céleste stood firm. "Not for a so young ladee," she announced implacably. "Eet ees not *convenable*." And that was that.

Not yet being out, Mariah could not be invited to any formal gatherings, but there were sufficient informal occasions, small parties, and sorties where she could display her charms. Her youth was betrayed by her unbridled enjoyment in everything: the dancing, the food, the company, especially the company. It came as a jolt to Trixie to think that when she was younger she might have acted the way Mariah was acting now. Had she burst into impulsive speech, engaged anyone, whether she had been introduced or not, and twirled with uncontrolled enthusiasm on the dance floor, just as Mariah was now doing? For the first time, she began to see what her mild governess had meant.

"You mustn't be quite so *loud*, Mariah," said Trixie, feeling like a governess herself, the morning after an evening when Mariah's voice had seemed to come from everywhere. "Everyone likes to see high spirits, but not so much that they positively overwhelm one. A lady should *add* to the pleasure of the group, not attempt to be the only source of it. And you *must* stop ogling any presentable male who enters the room! And really, one would think you were starved the way you consumed those lemon creams at supper."

Luckily, after her confidences in the park, Mariah thought Trixie knew everything and was prepared to listen to her. As a consequence, she began to acquire a little more of what Uncle Leonard called *town bronze*, much to Trixie's satisfaction. The Countess's indolent egotism prevented her from noticing anything amiss in her daughter's behavior.

As for Margarethe, she was enjoying herself as much as Mariah, though her demeanor remained as calm as ever. She could see that women in London enjoyed a great deal more freedom than they had in her homeland. She became accustomed to Trixie's enthusiastic energy and bold way of expressing herself. She did it with such charm, no one was offended.

When she mentioned this to her mother, the Baroness commented sagely, "Of course, she is a wealthy young woman, and what is considered becoming in her would not in a woman less well endowed. Her young cousin, for example, is more likely to be criticized than applauded."

Margarethe digested that. "And tell me, Mama, do you think it right for me to read these novels Trixie has given me? I confess I find them exciting, but are they altogether *proper*?"

"Oh, there's no harm in them," replied her Mama equally sagely, "so long as you understand it is pure fiction. I know you have much too much sense to confuse them with real life."

"Of course, Mama. I know that! They are nothing more than an entertainment!"

"I knew we understood each other," said the Baroness.

Chapter Ten

London was also making a marked impression on Chauncey. He knew he was his mother's favorite, and had always been happy enough to indulge her. It had suited him to adopt the artistically poetic air that pleased her. But now, meeting his college friends in London and accompanying his sister and Margarethe around the park, he was intent on becoming a man about town. The cause of it all was, ironically enough, the showy slug his Uncle Leonard had procured for him.

Chauncey was, as Leonard had said, a cow-fisted rider, but the grey his uncle had bought not only looked good but adapted well to his riding style. The horse's insensitive mouth did not jib at being tugged and pulled. Both man and beast were lazy, and though the grey was good-natured enough to trot and even canter on occasion, he did not willingly gallop. But since Chauncey rarely asked him to do so, there was perfect understanding between them.

In fact, few of the group of young blades he fell in with galloped. They were too concerned with keeping their intricately tied neckcloths in place and their shirt collar points as stiff as possible. Nothing was more fatal to one's appearance than a wild gallop. And of course, riding in the park they were much more concerned with ogling the young ladies.

If they wanted more excitement, their larks usually involved riding into the country and drinking a good deal more than was good for them, then being chased by the Watch when they returned rowdily to town. Since the man was on foot and they on horseback, they had no difficulty in evading capture.

More than once Chauncey had recently crept up to his room in a condition he would have described as *just a trifle bosky*. His mother, seeing her darling boy escaping her cloying affections, took him to task.

"I do think you should have some consideration for my nerves," she chided him mournfully one afternoon after a particularly riotous evening that kept him out well into the small hours. "I barely slept a wink last night, I was so anxious about you!"

She didn't mention the creams she had consumed in great quantities at dinner despite her frequent complaints that they gave her indigestion.

"Oh Lord, Mama!" he replied, "I'm not a baby. I'm well able to look after myself. Uncle has given me a key and I told old Trowbridge not to wait up. He left a candle and tinder box for me on the hall table."

"The church clock had stuck three before I heard you stumbling upstairs," she continued, ignoring his protests. "And look at you! The afternoon is almost over and only now do you come down. I suppose you've been asleep all this time!"

"For goodness sake, Mama, a chap's got to have a little fun! The Lord knows, there'll be none at all once I go back up to Oxford for the second year. Can't say I'm looking forward to it! By the by," he added nonchalantly, "I'm going to write to Papa and ask him if he'll lend me the blunt for a phaeton and pair. All the fellows have them. I'll repay him next quarter. I'll be up by then with nothing to spend my money on."

His doting Mama gave a shriek and was only revived by Chauncey's quick proffering of the smelling salts never far from her side.

"A... *a phaeton!*" she exclaimed. "You'll turn it over and kill yourself!" Words failed her. She sank back against the cushions, her breast heaving. "My heart!" she moaned. "It can't stand the strain! I already have palpitations thinking about it! If you buy a phaeton, I shall die! I forbid you to ask your father for money for such a purpose! I shall write and tell him not to give it to you!"

Chauncey had lived with his mother's heart all his life. That's why he instinctively reached for the *sal volatile*. But this was the first time he didn't bend over her solicitously.

Instead he exploded, "Really, Mother, you can't expect a chap to give up a good time with his friends because his Mama has palpitations!" Then, to add insult to injury, he added, "After all, you've had palpitations any time these last twenty years and yet you're still here! Write to my father if you choose. I shall manage!"

At this unfilial outburst, for the first time in her life Lady Shelby fell into a paroxysm of real tears and had to be helped to her bed by her maid. But Chauncey didn't care. Seething with indignation, he'd already left.

Still pursuing her aim of throwing her uncle and Cornelius together with the Baroness and Margarethe, a few days later, Trixie made up a group for an intimate dinner. With the uneven numbers in the combined families there were five ladies and only three gentlemen, so to round out the party, she asked her uncle to invite his old friend Arthur Witherspoon and his son Arno, whom they often met in the park.

It was thus an oddly mixed-age group that sat down to eat: Uncle Leonard, Witherspoon Senior, Lady Shelby, and the Baroness at one end, with Trixie, Margarethe, Mariah, Cornelius, Arno, and Chauncey at the other. At one point it had seemed that Lady Shelby, still suffering from the rebuff her son had given her, would refuse to be of the number, claiming exhaustion and an inability to dine in company.

Trixie went up to see her and very soon discovered the problem. She confronted her cousin.

"Go and apologize to your Mama instantly, Chauncey," she commanded. "I refuse to have our dinner party spoiled by your foolish quarrel."

When he declared he would not, she rounded on him. "I declare, how childish you are, to be sure! Here our uncle has provided you with every facility, including a...," she was going to say *fine* but knew perfectly well her uncle's opinion of the animal, "... a *good-looking* horse, and you do not have the manners to do him this small service. You are like a child who has been deprived of a sugar plum!"

Then she had a momentary pang of sympathy for him. Everyone knew his mother was a trial, and she thanked her lucky stars fate had put her in the hands of her uncle instead of her aunt. "Look, just quickly say you're sorry and then tell your Mama you have asked Cook to prepare hazelnut creams specially for her. That should persuade her."

Chauncey was in fact suffering from the guilt of knowing he had ignored his mother's wish and had just that morning purchased a high-perch phaeton and a spirited pair to go with it. He was to pick it up the following afternoon. On top of that, the idea that Trixie, whom he admired, thought him nothing more than a child filled him with almost tearful vexation. He made a muttered apology to his mother, and she, persuaded as much by the hazelnut creams as by the joy in her favorite child returning to the fold, agreed to come down to dinner. In the event, she wore one of her new gowns and, enjoying the compliments as much as the dessert, passed an agreeable evening.

Chauncey, on the other hand, continued to look vexed and glum, so much so that Margarethe drew him aside after the meal and asked him what the problem was. He told her the story, omitting the detail about having purchased the phaeton.

She listened sympathetically and said, "But you must derive satisfaction in knowing you did the right thing in apologizing to your dear mother. To be sure, it is irksome to be treated as a child, but I fancy you have shown her you are one no longer. You have proven yourself a man."

Her words fell like balm on his ears. "Do you really think so?"

"Of course. She will respect you the more."

Chauncey seized her hands and kissed them fervently. "You are an angel!" he said.

His sister happened to look towards him at that moment and both saw the kisses and heard the exclamation. Her romantic heart, fed by the novels that were her daily diet, was filled with emotion.

Trixie missed the moment entirely, observing her uncle with the Baroness. He was looking his best, handsome and dapper in a new coat that fit him to perfection. It had been a stroke of genius, she thought, to invite Arthur Witherspoon. Nothing could have formed a greater contrast. Mr. Witherspoon wore an old coat that had probably been fashionable twenty years before. She had seen him in it countless times over the years. Instead of the swallow tail that looked so elegant, it had a sort of skirt in the back. His waistcoat was long and close-buttoned compared with those sported by her uncle and the younger men which were high cut and with wide lapels. The whole ensemble looked dusty and worn. Was he so impecunious he couldn't afford a new coat? She didn't think so. Arno, who was making Mariah laugh on the other side of the salon, always looked well turned out.

Cornelius had fixed himself to her side, where he was regaling her with an account of his trip to the Elgin Marbles. "I tell you, Trixie, it's all a hum! Most of the statues are missing arms or legs or even their heads! What's the use of a headless statue, I ask you? Can't even see what the feller looked like." The caryatids designed to support the temple came in for special scorn. "Everyone was raving about those women with the trays on their heads, but half of them are missing their arms or half their faces! And I don't know what they're doing with those trays anyway. Couldn't be for carrying a drink – they would be too high for a chap to reach. And they charge you sixpence to get in! Lord Elgin is a regular gulling cove!"

Being familiar with Corny's colorful language, Trixie understood this to mean a *cheat*. She laughed. "Good thing everyone doesn't feel as you do, Corny. He needs the funds. I've heard he's already washed-up and his wife is leaving him! Anyway, go and ask Margarethe to play for us. You know how you enjoy it!"

He looked at her a little strangely, but being accustomed to doing what she wanted, he went willingly enough. The evening ended with the young people around the pianoforte with Margarethe. Trixie was well pleased.

Chapter Eleven

Lukas von Schwerin's interview with the estate manager Mr. Goodwin went better than expected.

"It's like this, sir," said Goodwin. "I tried to do what needed doing, but, meaning no disrespect, your grandfather wasn't himself these last months, or even longer. When his lady died, the stuffing seemed to go out of him. He'd listen with half an ear, and I'd think he'd agreed to summat, but when I told him how I was getting along with it he'd look at me as if it was the first he'd heard of it and tell me to stop. That's why the roofs of the cottages along the north road there is only half done, the sheep pens is half empty and we've got fields lying fallow as should be a-growing. I'm sorry, sir, but that's the way it's been."

"I can see that," said Lukas. "He must have known things were slipping away from him and been afraid to lose control. Poor man. I wish I could have been here to help him."

"He spoke of you often, sir. He'd say you was doing your duty by your family over there, and he couldn't ask for more. But he missed you."

"And I missed him."

Lukas was silent for a few moments, thinking of the happy days he'd spent here as a boy. Then he shook himself.

"Still, no good crying over what might have been. We must look to the future. Let's go over the whole estate and make lists: immediate needs, needs for next year and needs for the future."

"Gladly, sir, and may I say what a pleasure it will be to see the old place put back together."

Lukas and Goodwin inspected every inch of the estate. Having seen the dilapidated state of the cottages, Lukas determined that the immediate need was for those to be repaired before the winter set in. He told Goodwin to order whatever was necessary. The meager harvest had been brought in and the lambs sold, so the tenant farmers would have the time to renovate their homes once they had the materials. Many of the cottages had been there the nearly two hundred years the farm had been in operation. The sheep pens would need repair, as would the hay barns. Sheep are hardy animals and can crop grass through snow, but supplemental fodder is necessary, especially during prolonged icy periods.

It was obvious the harvest was insufficient for both men and beasts. To remedy the situation, Lukas rode around to all the neighboring estates, often away for days at a time, begging to buy wheat for the workers and fodder for the animals, and then helping organize cart convoys to bring it in.

Then Lukas and Goodwin discussed the crop rotation of wheat, ryegrass, oats and barley for human and animal consumption. During this time it became clear that the estate was still using a few old wooden ploughs. These needed a team of at least four oxen to pull them through the heavy clay soil. The more modern metal-wheeled and bladed ploughs were much lighter and could be pulled by a pair of animals. He wondered at that, for although, by and large, farming methods were more advanced in England than back in the German provinces, wooden ploughs were a thing of the past nearly everywhere in Europe. When he spoke of it to Mr. Goodwin, he had his answer.

"It's all due to some of the older farmers not wanting to change to the new metal ploughs when they first come out, sir. They was used to what they did and how they did it. It's always the same. Then with the wars, the young men was gone, and besides, everything was so expensive. There wasn't the metal to be had to make the mouldboards. The smith was willing, but he couldn't get the materials."

"Well, if we can buy or make new ploughs before the spring it will help in two ways. For one, we can sell or slaughter several pairs of oxen and not have to feed them over the winter. They will feed us. If we start looking now, we should be able to have them by ploughing time."

Lukas drove the gig he habitually took back to Chorley House puzzling over the work ahead. Juno, lying at his feet, sighed in sympathy.

Chapter Twelve

With all the work needing to be set in motion, it was almost two months before Lukas could think about returning to London. He was anxious to do so. Letters he had received from his mother and sister worried him a little. Since the death of his father he had become accustomed to making all the decisions for the family. But in his absence, things seemed to have run out of his control.

First, there was the matter of his mother's carriage. The von Schwerins had arrived in London in a convoy of three coaches hired in Dover for the conveyance to London of the family, the servants, and the luggage. They had been forced to sell their own coaches before crossing the channel, no ferry being prepared to ship such cumbersome vehicles and their teams. In fact, it had been no great loss, they all agreed, as they would never have been able to use the antiquated vehicles in London. Compared with the smart turn-outs they saw, theirs would have appeared ridiculous.

Lukas' first imperative had been to settle his mother and sister in the family townhouse. But then he had been anxious to get to Chorley House as soon as possible. He had taken a quick look in Tattersall's, meaning to buy a smart carriage for the ladies and something suitable for himself. He had found the latter quite quickly: a nice-looking curricle and a neat pair to go with it, being sold by a gentleman whose pockets were to let following disastrous losses at gambling. But he considered none of the carriages on offer suitable for his mother.

He had been inclined towards a landaulet until a smart gentleman told him that these days barouches were preferable. Landaulets were hopelessly passé. Not being familiar with London fashion, Lukas had taken his advice, but no barouches were on offer in the short week he had to spend in the capital. In the end, his mother had told him she could well wait until he returned. He had gone off in the curricle, never imagining he would be away so long. Nevertheless, when he received the following letter from his mother, he was not best pleased.

> My dear Lukas,
>
> The infrequent nature of your correspondence tells me more than your words do that you are dreadfully busy. Poor boy! I wish I had come with you. I could have surely taken some of the weight from your shoulders.
>
> It seems so unfair that Margarethe and I should be enjoying the delights of the capital while you are working so hard. For delights there are!
>
> We have seen the Elgin Marbles, accompanied there by the charming Mrs. Wolfson and her son Cornelius, a pleasant though rather empty-headed young man. Luckily there was a pamphlet to explain it all, as otherwise, I'm afraid we would have been rather in the dark. We also very much enjoyed Edmund Kean in Hamlet but we have found the opera rather too, let us say, opulent for our taste.
>
> I must tell you that Mr. Leonard Shelby, the uncle of a young lady we met at a dancing party (you see how

gay we are!) who is fast becoming Margarethe's best friend, has guided me in the purchase of a barouche and pair. We are delighted with it and I trust you will be, too.

Both your sister and I miss you very much and are eager for your return.

I hope you are sleeping better, my poor boy. I pray for you every night,

Your loving Mother

Of course, he was happy his mother and sister were enjoying life. It is what he wished for them. But the mention of this Cornelius who had taken them to the Marbles disturbed him. If he had invited the ladies there without first informing himself about the antiquities, he must be a man of no sense. He hoped Margarethe was not too taken with him. Then this Shelby who presumed, on what must be a short acquaintance, to help his mother purchase a carriage, what kind of man was he? Lukas usually trusted his mother's judgement, but she might have been taken in.

A couple of weeks later he received a missive from his sister that made him worry even more.

Dear Brother,

Mama has told me how busy you are. We both worry about you and long for you to be with us.

We are going along very well. We have been lucky enough to form a friendship with Lady Beatrix Shelby who knows everyone and introduces us everywhere. Hardly a day goes by without an invitation of some sort or another.

Perhaps you would find little pleasure in dancing and parties, and it is not to be wondered at after the years you have spent, but I must say I am finding London society delightful!

Guess what! I have been presented at Almack's. I missed the presentation at court, since it happened before we came to London. In any case, my friend Trixie said it was a lot of bother for nothing. But she insisted that I make my début at Almack's. I wore a new silk gown of the palest pink which was very pretty. Lady Beatrix had her modiste make it for me. I do not want to boast, but I think I looked very well. Trixie says Almack's is the place one must be seen if one wishes to find a husband.

This seems to be the desire of all the heroines in some very interesting novels she has given me to read. Or at least, the desire to find a young and handsome husband, and hopefully one with a fortune too! I have never read novels before and am enjoying them very much.

Mother and I miss you and long for you to return. I can't wait to present my handsome brother to my friends!

Come back soon!

Your loving sister,

Margarethe

This letter worried Lukas a good deal more than his mother's had done. The Margarethe he knew was a quiet, serious girl, and had no thought in her head of marriage or novels. In fact, he considered it his duty to find a good husband for her. He had no time at all for the ideas of the young English women he had met. They seemed bold and indelicate in their talk. The concept of *falling in love* was ridiculous to him. Marriages should be arranged between families of like status and expectations. Otherwise they were doomed to failure. His return to London was clearly long overdue.

The problem now arose as to what to do with his grandfather's old dog, Juno. He didn't want to leave her, but it didn't seem fair to take her away from the only home she'd ever known. She had climbed onto his bed beside him the first night he was there, seeming to sense his need. She comforted him when he was shaken awake by visions of the dead and dying, and always, always, that smell of blood. She would lick his face and put her head on his heaving chest. During the day she stuck to his side and, if instead of taking the gig around the estate, Lukas rode one of the saddle horses, she would follow him until her chest was heaving and her tongue hanging to the ground. In the beginning, Lukas had ignored her once or twice and continued on his way, only to find the dog plodding towards him as he returned at the end of the day, miles from home. After that, he took the gig and Juno lay there peacefully, her head on Lukas's foot.

He decided it was best to lock her in the kitchen when the time came for his departure. The kitchen, with its good smells and promise of tidbits, must be every dog's dream. Lukas was sure that once there, she would forget about him and settle down.

But Juno had other ideas. She knew something was afoot when she saw Lukas packing his clothes into the large bag he had brought with him. He had brought a minimum, for he had not expected to stay so long. He only had his linen, a second coat and another pair of boots. Juno knew this was not what he normally took with him around the estate and was very suspicious when Lukas enticed her down to the kitchen and shut her in.

For a while she lay next to the hearth, but her ears were cocked. She heard the clatter of the curricle and pair being brought around from the stable. She got up and stood by the back door whining softly.

"Now, now, Juno," said Mrs. Truly, coming into the kitchen and depositing a pile of rags made from worn sheets that had finally become too thin for use, "you stay here like a good girl. The Master has to go to London but you'll be here along of us, as always."

As soon as she left, Juno did something she'd known how to do for a long time. She put her front paws up on the door and with her nose nudged under the wooden latch that lifted the crossbar holding the door closed. In seconds, she was outside and running after the curricle as it bowled down the road. It was good luck that Lukas had to slow down to a walk as a farmer with his cart plodded around the bend.

"Lookee, Master. There's yer old bitch a-running down the road," announced the farmer. "She wants to go along a' you as usual, seemingly."

For the estate people were by now well accustomed to Juno going everywhere with Lukas. Lukas looked back and sighed. He reined in his horses to a complete stop and waited for her to catch up. He knew it was no good. Short of tying the faithful old lady up, there was no way he could keep her from following. She'd keep going till she dropped.

"Up you get then, you silly old thing," he said as Juno came alongside. She gave a bound and settled in the bottom of the curricle, her tongue hanging out.

"I'm happy you're coming, to tell you the truth," Lukas told her. "The servants will probably find you a damned nuisance and my mother won't like you lying in front of the fire like some moldy old rug. But I'll be glad you're there."

Juno had closed her eyes. *London? What's that?* she thought. But she couldn't be bothered to puzzle it out, and simply fell asleep.

Chapter Thirteen

Lukas von Schwerin trotted along at a steady gait aimed at not tiring the horses. He was pondering the news he had received just before leaving, that one of the tenant farms had become vacant. A son of a long time tenant had returned to the farm he had grown up in. His older brother had worked it along with his father but he had always been army mad, and when he had the opportunity, he had signed up. Unfortunately, he had been killed in action at Corunna. The old man had finally realized he couldn't manage by himself, and the younger boy, who had gone off on his own account, had agreed to come back. His own place was consequently empty.

With the number of men killed in action over the last twelve years, and the departure of farm laborers into the factories that provided a regular wage uninterrupted by weather or blight, it was not easy to find a replacement. Lost in his thoughts, Lukas only vaguely took note of a rider coming towards him out of the trees and was entirely unprepared for the man to come to a halt in the middle of the road, level what looked like a musket at him, and shout, "Stand and Deliver!"

Lukas reined in his horses and before he could stop her, Juno leaped out of the curricle and ran barking towards the horseman.

The man pointed his firearm at the running dog and prepared to fire. Lukas, who had seen too much robbery and violence on the road during the retreat from Moscow to ever travel again without a firearm, withdrew a pistol from the capacious pocket of his driving cloak and fired.

The man's firearm leaped from his hand, he swayed and fell from his horse. Juno caught up with the attacker and would have buried her teeth in him, had Lukas not called, "Down, Juno, down!" The dog immediately sat down but growled menacingly every time the man made a move.

Lukas clicked up his horses and walked them to Juno and the fallen attacker. He had a kerchief around his mouth and nose, and his hat pulled well over his eyes. His firearm lay at some distance from him. Lukas picked it up and looked at it. It was a musket, like many he had seen in battle.

"Looks like army issue," he said to the man on the ground. "Why are you using it like this, soldier?"

The man squinted up at him. "You try earning an honest living, yer honor, in times like these. I've got a wife and son to provide for."

"Are you hurt?"

"Nah, just the skin off me fingers. I ain't never seen shooting like it." The man held up his bleeding hand, and Juno growled. "Good bitch yer got there, I'd say."

"Yes, she is," said Lukas shortly. He held out his hand and helped the man to his feet. "Take off your hat and that thing around your face and let me look at you."

The man removed the kerchief and his hat and stood before Lukas. He was about thirty, thin to the point of emaciation, with sandy colored hair and light blue eyes that met Lukas' gaze squarely. His face showed lines of strain and blood dripped from his hand to the dusty road.

Lukas reached for the canteen of water that was another thing he never traveled without. He remembered the raging thirst of blindingly hot days when men and horses had suffered for lack of plain water. The Russians would poison the wells with the carcasses of dead animals as they retreated, rather than leave them for the enemy.

He took the man's hand. The fingertips had been scored and were bleeding profusely. The smell of it made Lukas's gorge rise, but he fought it down and poured water over the wounds. Then he took the man's kerchief and tied it securely around his fingers.

"What's your name, soldier, and where did you see action?"

The man sketched a rather wobbly salute. "Private Albert Potter, sir. I were in the 73rd Foot at Waterloo, under Lieutenant-Colonel Harris. More than half of us lost or wounded. Then we comes home and no jobs to be had."

"Well, Private Potter, I don't like to see a soldier acting like a highwayman. Have you any experience as a farmer or shepherd?"

"I've never dealt with no sheep, but my missus was born and raised on a farm. I had casual work there on an off for four seasons, so I knows me way around. I took to soldiering when we married and she started a baby. I needed more reg'lar work."

"Then take this." Lukas scribbled on a visiting card he took from his inside pocket and gave it to his would-be attacker. "Go to Chorley House. It's not more than seven miles back up that way. Ask to be shown the way to the estate manager, a man by the name of Goodwin. Give him this card and he'll show you a farm that needs a tenant. If you think you can take it on, get your family and come back. You'll pay no land rent until after the first harvest. Let's see what you can do. And take this to help you along. He handed the man a roll of money. I'd rather give it to you than have it stolen."

The soldier stood stock still, staring down at the paper and the money, then up at Lukas, as if unable to believe his eyes. "I... I ain't much at reading," he said to Lukas at last. "Please to tell me your name so I knows who to thank. And thank you, I do, sir, You won't regret it. Me and the missus will work our fingers to the bone to be worthy of what you're doing for us."

He made as if to kiss Lukas's hand, but Juno growled, so he took a step back. He stood up straight and saluted. Lukas saluted in return, saying "Lukas von Schwerin." He lowered his hand. "And you'd better take this." He gave the man his musket. "Just don't use it on anything with two legs. The war is over, thank God."

Then he called to Juno. Man and dog climbed up into the curricle, Lukas clicked up the horses and trotted away.

Private Potter, late of His Majesty's Army, stood looking at his back as he disappeared down the road. "My God," he said "I didn't understand a word of his name, but if he'd said the Archangel Gabriel, I wouldn't a been surprised."

Chapter Fourteen

In London, Chauncey had taken possession of his high perch phaeton at Tattersall's. When he had climbed aboard the vehicle as it stood for sale in the yard, he had not realized how far from the horses he would be once they were poled up. He had nearly no experience of driving a pair. He gave the reins a timid shake. The greys snorted and tossed their heads but did not move. He shook them a bit harder and said *Walk On*, as he would have said to the old horse pulling the gig he was used to at home. Something must have penetrated the pairs' combined intelligence, and they moved forward, jerking immediately into a trot.

It was lucky they appeared to know the way out of the yard, for it would be an exaggeration to say that Chauncey was in any sort of control of the vehicle. The horses made up their own minds as to the direction they wished to go, but since this was back into the center of London where they had formerly been housed, it suited Chauncey very well.

Tattersall's was on the corner of Hyde Park, in a semi-rural area, and the traffic was at first light. Once he was a little calmer, Chauncey was able to pull the horses back into a walk and then timidly flick at the leader's ear with the hugely long whip he had brought with him, to urge them back to a trot.

He practiced this two or three times, and by the time he was in the traffic of central London he was quite pleased with himself, though had yet to master the manipulation of the whip. He was certainly was not able to let it fly out then catch the thong as it returned, as he had seen the members of the Four Horse Club do. He wondered if his Uncle Leonard would instruct him, but he knew the poor opinion his uncle had of his horsemanship and hardly dared ask him.

When they arrived in Mayfair, the horses turned towards their old address, and Chauncey had the devil of a job redirecting them. He most certainly was not going to attempt to turn the phaeton around in the street. He ended up going in quite the wrong direction for some time, until he persuaded them to turn down side streets and go around in a square till they were heading the right way. He was hot and bothered when he finally drew up in front of his uncle's tall town house.

He tried to compose himself before descending, and succeeded well enough to be able to enter the house with a reasonable show of nonchalance. It was unlucky that his mother was crossing the hall as the wide front door opened. She saw the phaeton. Aghast, she dropped everything she was holding. A *Mode Illustrée,* a silk shawl and the inevitable bottle of smelling salts fell to the stone floor, where the bottle broke and filled the air with an acrid scent that brought tears to the footmen's eyes.

Ignoring it all, she threw herself against her son's breast, causing him to stagger, for the daily consumption of creams was not without its consequences on her figure.

"No! No! No!" she screeched, "Oh, my son, I forbid it! Do not kill your mother by traveling in that... that *devil's machine,* I implore you!"

Chauncey, embarrassed by his mother's screeching, his nerves already overwrought by the trip he had just made and the acrid scent of *sal volatile* in his throat, replied with heat, "And I implore *you*, Mama, to cease this display immediately! It is beyond enough when a man may not choose his own means of conveyance! I had hoped you would by now have accustomed yourself to the idea of a simple phaeton!"

"A simple phaeton! It is a death machine! I shall never accustom myself to you driving such a thing! Never!"

"In that case, I shall leave you! I shall go to where I am understood and appreciated. Fear not, I shall not darken your door again!"

And with that statement, which would have done credit to a character in one of the novels Mariah so enjoyed, he stormed out the front door, leaving his mother, sunken into a heap in the middle of the hall, sobbing and holding out her arms to him. It was a magnificently dramatic scene.

His sister had run partway down the stairs when the screeching began and heard his parting remark. She now went to support her mother, who might indeed have genuinely fainted from the shock, had not the liberally distributed smelling salts prevented it. Into this affecting image of mother and daughter walked the Lady Beatrix, returning from a duty visit to an old retainer and sublimely unaware of the horrors that had just been perpetrated.

Chapter Fifteen

Meanwhile, Lukas had arrived at the family townhouse in Mayfair. He jumped down from the curricle with Juno at his heels, throwing the reins to one of the boys who loitered on the linkway to earn a few pence by performing just that service.

He mounted the front steps and hammered on the knocker.

"Baron, sir!" exclaimed the elderly servant who opened the door. He was one of those who had come with them from Germany.

"Fritz! Good to see you," said Lukas, shaking the hand of the old retainer. "Is my mother in the drawing room?"

"No, sir. She is from home. She left yesterday. With her maid."

"But didn't she receive my note that I was returning to London?"

"I think not, Baron. A letter arrived just a few minutes ago written in your hand addressed to the Baroness. Naturally, I did not open it. It's there on the hall table."

Lukas picked up the letter and saw the problem. In his haste he had written the direction very poorly and it had obviously been delivered at first to the wrong address.

"Where has she gone?"

"I'm afraid I cannot say, sir."

"Did she say when she would be back?"

"No sir, but her maid had some bags. I gathered they would be gone some while."

"Did my sister accompany her?"

"No, Baron. Fraülein Margarethe left today not long ago. She was picked up by a young man in a smart carriage. She had two or three bandboxes with her. She was in something of a hurry. I don't know where she was going."

"What young man?" Lukas could feel his temper rising. He did his best to control it.

"I'm afraid I cannot say, sir."

"Was her maid with her?"

"No, sir."

The information might have been more complete had the regular butler been there. But the Baroness had given him and most of the other servants the day off, and the old majordomo from Mecklenburg-Schwerin was less proficient in English than he liked to admit. He misunderstood most of what he heard. Lukas spoke to him in German, of course.

"What in heaven's name is going on here?" Lukas was more enraged by the minute. Juno heard the anger in his voice and growled. Lukas put his hand on the dog's head. "My mother is from home, heaven knows where, and my sister has gone off with a young man carrying bandboxes but taking no maid. Does that sound like usual behavior to you?"

"No, sir. Back at home it would be most unusual. But here in London, sir, I have remarked that the young people seem to, er, intermingle much more. Customs are much freer, it seems. It is the same with dogs," he added, looking at Juno with dislike. "At home we do not allow such dogs in the house."

"Perhaps not, but this is England, and people have a different relationship with their animals. But I did not believe the behavior of young ladies to be so very different. Find her maid and ask where she has gone and with whom."

"Her maid isn't here, sir. Most of the servants have been given the day off. The Baroness knows she can rely on me."

Lukas was by now seething. "Do you know the names of any of my sister's friends? Think, man! Someone must know where she is!"

"She is often in the company of a Lady Beatrix, sir. A most charming young lady, if I may say."

Lukas remembered the name from Margarethe's letter.

"Yes, I understand she enjoys the freedom of conduct you referred to just now. If anyone knows the reason for this extraordinary behavior it will be she. Find me someone who can give me the direction of Lady Beatrix Shelby. Be quick about it!"

A few minutes later, furnished with Trixie's address by one of the footmen who had carried frequent notes between the two houses, Lukas was driving his tired horses through the streets of London, with Juno again at his feet, her nose on his boots. He was running over Margrethe's letter over in his mind, remembering the references to this Beatrix Shelby, her advice about Almack's and husbands and the "interesting" novels she had given his sister. He ground his teeth. She had obviously been filling his sister's head with arrant nonsense. His temper, which he had to work hard to control these days, was fully aroused by the time he arrived at the Shelby townhouse.

The débacle caused by Chauncey's phaeton was now over. Lady Shelby had been carried up to her room by two of the unfortunate footmen who were beginning to wonder whether the excellent wages their employer paid them were worth the backbreaking exercise imposed on them. She was moaning gently on her bed as her maid wafted burned feathers under her nose.

Trixie and Mariah were in the salon. Having fully thrashed out the question as to whether Chauncey was wise or foolish to ignore his Mama, and whether he would indeed break his neck with his ridiculous new vehicle, they were now engaged in a lively discussion of the appearance of various female members of the ton at the last ball. Mariah had been particularly struck by one dashing lady, not quite in her first youth, appearing in scarlet silk with pink roses. She declared she would like just such a gown for herself. "Tasteless" was Trixie's estimation, a position she held to in spite of Mariah's hot denials.

They were therefore astonished when the door opened and a tall, commanding figure came in, followed by the flustered butler who blurted out, "The Baron von Schwerin." Normally a placid man with an air of authority, he had not been able to withstand the angry Lukas with a growling dog at his side, who had simply strode past him, demanding to see the Lady Beatrix at once.

The two ladies stared at their visitor in wonder. Lukas von Schwerin was extremely good-looking in a stern, square-jawed way. Like his sister, he was very fair but whereas her eyes were of a pale blue, his were piercingly so. He looked exactly like the hero of a Romance.

He was dressed with perfect propriety and even style, but not quite in the London mode. He was in riding boots, not normally acceptable in a drawing room, his long dark green cloak was fastened at the top and thrown back over his broad shoulders to reveal a well-cut wool riding coat, sober waistcoat, and breeches. The points of his shirt collar were conservative, as was his neckcloth. And a large yellow dog was at his side. It was clearly a gun dog, and not the sort of animal generally seen in the salons of Mayfair.

It is not too much to say he took their breath away. For Mariah, he seemed to have walked right out of one of her novels. He was tall, strong, and handsome. His faithful hound by his side, he looked ready to rescue any maiden from distress, no matter how hideous. Trixie's reaction was more primal. She felt a lurch in her stomach she had never experienced before. She felt herself flushing; she caught her breath. For the first time in her life it was not her head that reacted to a man, but her whole being.

Chapter Sixteen

The visitor clicked his heels. "Lukas von Schwerin," he said in perfectly fluent English. "Have I the honor to address Lady Beatrix Shelby?" He bowed stiffly towards her.

The clicking of the heels brought Trixie to her senses. Her emotions already out of kilter, she had an almost overwhelming desire to laugh. It was so like the performance she had enacted for her uncle. Controlling herself, she stood and curtseyed formally.

"I am Beatrix Shelby," she said and lifted her eyes. "And what a handsome animal! What is her name?" She held out her hand towards Juno.

Thus, Lukas's first impression of Trixie was of an attractive young woman with laughter in her dancing brown eyes, smiling at his dog. But he was too angry to appreciate her charms and was astonished when Juno went forward, her tail wagging, and gave Trixie's proffered hand a brief lick.

"Her name is Juno and like others under your influence," said Lukas coldly, "she seems to have forgotten her manners. Heel, Juno." The dog immediately returned to his side.

Trixie was taken aback, but before she could speak their visitor continued, "I have just returned to town from my estate in the country, and I find my family missing. My mother's absence is perhaps easily explained, as she seems to have left with her maid. I must assume the trip was planned, however little the staff seem to know about it. But my sister appears to have left at short notice with a young man in a smart conveyance carrying bandboxes but with no maid. This is altogether inexplicable."

He hesitated for a moment, then continued. "I understand from her letters that you, Lady Shelby, have been the chief influence in her life these last months, an influence I had already begun to deplore, even before this extraordinary behavior. It appeared that you were encouraging her to behave in a way inconsistent with her upbringing. I am therefore hoping you can enlighten me. Where is Margarethe?"

Trixie was stunned. She felt a strong physical attraction to this man, and here he was, looking at her with extreme dislike and blaming her for whatever he believed Margarethe to have done. In a moment, her rage boiled to the surface.

"I cannot imagine why you should impute to me any sort of behavior from Margarethe, and I very much resent your accusation. It is a pity I am not a man, when I could show you exactly how much I resent it," she replied, barely able to control herself. "I am not Margarethe's keeper. I have no idea where she may be or how or why she went there. There. You have your answer. You may now leave. I have no appetite for your insults."

"My sister never strayed an inch from the precepts of her upbringing until she came to London and met you," replied Lukas, working hard to control his anger.

"If what you say about her departure is true, I confess I am myself astonished by such behavior on her part. I had not thought it of her. But then, why should I be surprised, since I have now experienced your own want of propriety. I have never before been subjected to such insult from any man, much less from one I have never met. If these are the manners that pertain where you come from, perhaps no one should be astonished by anything either of you do! In any case, I wish you good day!"

She stalked to the bell rope and was on the point of ringing for the butler when Mariah leaped to her feet and cried, "No, stop, Trixie! I know what's happened! It was Chauncey! She's eloped with Chauncey! He called her an angel and kissed her hands the other evening! I saw them! And I told you what he said when he left here after his argument with Mama! *I shall go to where I am understood and appreciated. Fear not, I shall not darken your door again!* Those were his exact words! He must have gone straight there with his new phaeton and persuaded her to elope with him! How romantic!"

She clasped her hands to her breast and looked at them with stars in her eyes.

Lukas took a furious step towards her. "What? What are you saying? Who are you and who is this Chauncey? Where did you see him kissing my sister's hands?"

Mariah gave a brief curtsey. "I am Trixie's, er Lady Shelby's cousin. Chauncey is my brother. I saw them here, at the dinner party last week!"

"Then it is as I said," Lukas turned to Trixie, his rage boiling over. "You have encouraged Margarethe to behave with an entire lack of propriety. And as for this Chauncey, by God, if I find he has compromised my sister in any way whatsoever, I'll kill him!"

"No!" shrieked Mariah! No, you can't kill my brother!"

"And you, his sister, consider an elopement *romantic*?" he shouted. "You are mad! It will be the ruin of her! It's clear you and Lady Beatrix are two of a kind! What kind of house is this?"

His raised voice caused Juno to emit a loud bark. This, together with Mariah's shrieking, brought the butler into the room, as hotfoot as his stately carriage would permit.

"Be quiet, all of you!" commanded Trixie. To the butler she said, "There is no problem, Foljambe, just a slight misunderstanding. Kindly send word to the stables to pole up my uncle's curricle and pair. I shall be needing them immediately."

"If you're sure, my lady," responded Foljambe, dubiously.

"Of course I'm sure! If my uncle were here he would give you the order himself. You know I am permitted to drive his bays."

Foljambe bowed and departed to give the order.

"What are you proposing to do?" asked Lukas, already ashamed of his outburst.

"I'm going after them, of course," replied Trixie. "I have no doubt of being able to overtake them. My uncle's bays are speedy and Chauncey is no whip. I doubt he can handle his cattle above a trot. Besides, I'll be surprised if he doesn't have them both in a ditch."

"It is not for you to chase after my sister," said the Baron, following her into the hall, with Juno at his heels.

"Keep your voice down, you fool," she replied. "You need not announce the affair to the whole household. Your sister concerns me less than my stupid cousin. You may leave this in my hands. After all, according to you, I am to blame for the whole thing. It will take me ten minutes to put on my riding clothes, then I shall be off."

She sketched a quick curtsey. "Goodbye, Baron. I'll bring Margarethe home, and after that, I sincerely hope I never lay eyes on you again."

Lukas' rage boiled up again. He wanted to forbid her to do anything in respect of his sister. But he knew the team he had ridden there would not be able to carry him anywhere else today. They were already tired. He was furious with his lack of choice, he was furious at being called a fool and he was furious that this woman he disliked had the upper hand.

"Then I shall go with you," he said, between his teeth. Seeing her ready to refuse, he added curtly, "Margarethe is my responsibility. If she has been as foolish as we imagine, she will listen to me more than to you. My team is too tired to go any further. In fact, they will need to be stabled." After a pause he added, "If you would be so kind."

It was Trixie's turn to hesitate. She knew what he said was true, and it would be easier if she had a man to accompany her, especially, though she hated to admit it, one as commanding as the Baron.

"Very well," she said. "If you insist." She turned and went upstairs to change.

Chapter Seventeen

While Trixie changed into her carriage dress, the Baron accompanied his horses to the mews stables at the back of the town house, with Juno still at his heels. A couple of terriers lived there to discourage the rats. They were lazing in the yard but stood up when Lukas and Juno came into view. They took a step towards the visitors, but Juno gave a low growl deep in her throat. It discouraged them; they dropped their ears and tails and slunk off into the shadows.

"Oh, Juno," said Lukas laughing in spite of his ill humor, "You seem determined to face my enemies for me. I could only wish you had not been so taken with Lady Beatrix. She's the worst of the lot!"

He went up to the head groom and began to tell him how he wanted his horses treated.

"Lord bless you, sir," said the head groom, "you don't need to worry! Mr. Shelby is very partic'lar 'bout his horses and we'll treat yours the same way, fine pair as they are, sir! Right as rain they'll be when you gets back, have no fear!" Then he took a step towards Juno. "Good protector you got there!" He made as if to pat her, but Juno gave another low growl.

"Juno! Behave!" said Lukas. "Don't mind her," he said to the groom. "She seems to think I need protecting."

"Nothing wrong with that, sir," replied the man. "Better that than those lap dogs the ladies have. Makes me fair sick to me stomach seeing them being fed tidbits when there's people starving!"

"Hmm." Lukas made no answer, knowing he was in the habit of doing exactly the same to Juno.

Man and dog watched as his horses were led away and the bays Trixie proposed driving were poled up to a smart curricle. They were clearly a spirited pair. The groom who drove the equipage to the front of the house had a little difficulty with them. Sitting next to him, with Juno in her usual position with her head on his boots, Lukas was tempted to take the reins.

He was therefore astonished when Lady Beatrix, who had taken no more than the ten minutes she had said she needed, came down the steps in front of the house and said crisply, "Thank you, Wood, I'll take them from here. No, there's no need for you to climb on the back. The Baron is no featherweight and an extra person will work the horses unnecessarily. He will give me any assistance I need." *I hope*, she added under her breath.

Carrying a matching cloak, Trixie was clad in a well-cut, fitted wool jacket and full skirt, in a shade of amber brown that perfectly matched her hair. A jaunty feathered bonnet was at a becoming angle on her head. She climbed nimbly into the vehicle. Juno had raised her head when she heard her voice and now gave her tail a whip of welcome. She patted her head. "Hello Juno," she said, "I know *you'll* help me, at any rate."

Lukas scowled. He knew the comment had been directed at him, but decided not to dignify it with a response. Trixie ignored him anyway. She clicked up the horses and they moved smoothy away.

It is not to be supposed that Uncle Leonard, the well-known whip, would have tolerated a ward who could not drive to an inch. In fact, from the moment she was put on a horse, Trixie had been a natural. She approached it all as great fun, was never afraid, and if she took a tumble only laughed. She had learned to drive a pair when she was much younger. It amused Uncle Leonard to have a mere girl drive him around the park while he lounged to one side, hailing his friends. Now, she expertly touched the leader's ear with the tip of her whip and caught the thong as it returned. Chauncey would have been mad with jealousy had he seen it.

Lukas was forced into grudging admiration as she deftly urged the bays into a trot and set off up the street at a smart gait. She navigated the traffic with easy nonchalance. This included a gig being driven by what looked like a parson, behind a barouche filled with fashionable ladies in enormous bonnets that was following an old-fashioned carriage that, in spite of being drawn by a full team, was lumbering along and holding up the entire train. Trixie dropped her hands and the bays surged forward, past all of them, missing by no more than a few inches a phaeton being driven towards them at a considerable clip.

"You took an unnecessary risk there," he remarked, as they settled back into a trot.

"On the contrary," she replied. "Speed is of the essence. It was therefore necessary. Besides, I know the bays and they know me. It's all a question of respect." She looked him straight in the eyes as she said this, and he felt himself forced to reply.

"I apologize, Lady Beatrix, if I spoke with too much heat earlier," said the Baron. "As a person with few responsibilities, I doubt you appreciate those I feel for my sister. She is new to London and may not have the experience or judgement necessary to navigate its shoals."

"Experience I give you, but judgement is another matter. I presume she knew she had no hope of your approving a match with Chauncey?"

"None whatsoever."

"Then apparently she seems to have been able to judge your prejudices to a tee. She was perfectly right when she thought you would discount out of hand a man she loved but you have never met."

"She loved!" he scoffed. "What can she know of love? Infatuation, perhaps. Do not tell me you approve of this match?" He looked at her in astonishment.

"A marriage between them in due course would not be such a disaster. Chauncey is too young at present, but he is heir to an Earldom and if he truly loves her, she could do a lot worse."

"Then why did you immediately set out to intercept them?"

"Because he is full young and easily led. I don't want him to make a mistake."

"You mean, you think *Margarethe* has led him on?" His voice rose.

"Who knows who led whom? They are both no doubt victims of romantic illusions. I'm sure Chauncey considers himself thwarted in his poetic and manly aspirations, and Margarethe has recently been reading novels. They may have had more influence on her than they should. Parents are so mistaken when they keep young women from those silly things. They should read as many as possible get it out of their system."

"I disagree entirely. If they are to be read, which I by no means admit, they should be read by older women with the wisdom to be able to distinguish reality from fantasy."

He was surprised when she retorted, "Tell me, Baron, have you ever read a novel?"

"Certainly not."

"Then, once again, you make a decision without being in possession of the facts. They are stupidly unrealistic, yes, but that's precisely why they should be read and discussed when women are in their formative years. If they can see the stories for what they are: pure fantasy without a grain of realism, that knowledge will add to the wisdom you talk about."

"Your cousin Mariah, whom I suppose to have absorbed this nonsense, declared this elopement *romantic*!"

"Yes, and on the face of it, so it is! But I know that a few minutes consideration will show her otherwise. You would be surprised at how *wise* she is regarding the opposite sex. We have often discussed it. The problem lies not with the novels but with a society that prefers to keep girls in total ignorance of the fundamental truths of relationships between the sexes. Women are led to believe that marriage is the only goal and yet they are completely unprepared for it!"

It was true that Mariah had frequently returned to their discussion that day in the park. Trixie knew she was not likely to do anything so foolish as an elopement, nor to enter into marriage without considering the character of the man she was to marry. Romance would not be the only consideration.

"And whence, may I ask, comes your own wisdom?" asked Lukas scornfully. "I estimate you and Margarethe to be of an age."

"From not being hemmed in by convention and custom. By being introduced early into mixed society where I could observe men in their natural element and not just through the lens of a matchmaking mama. I was lucky enough to live with my uncle, who thinks I can do just about anything he can."

"And you think all young women should have this freedom?"

"Certainly. No one thinks a boy of fifteen or sixteen needs to be protected from certain reading material or be so incapable of making sensible choices that all his actions have to be decided for him. In my estimation, given the same advantages of education, girls would be at least as *wise,* to use your word, as boys are. In fact, I would wager a fifteen year old girl, given the same advantages, would make better use of them."

Then we shall never agree," replied Lukas firmly. "Everything you say shows your own foolishness. I was right to lay the blame for Margarethe's behavior at your door. You have filled her head with this nonsense, and you may well have ruined her. Young women may have a good deal of sense, but their situation is so much more precarious. The sad truth is, in a moment of silliness, a young woman's good name is lost forever. Even if we are able to prevent this elopement, Margarethe and Chauncey may well have been seen together. He will be able to recover from it. She will not. Her whole future life will be a consequence of this foolish act. But if you do not see how fragile a woman's honor is, I cannot teach you."

A blistering retort sprang to Trixie's tongue, but they were encountering heavier traffic as they drove through the business district of the city, and she had to pay closer attention to what she was doing. So she said nothing, merely set her face and refused to look at him. He took the hint and they both traveled on in silence.

Chapter Eighteen

They were heading for *The Angel*, the staging Inn to the north of London, where coaches for Scotland could be boarded. It was possible Chauncey had left his phaeton there and they had taken the Stage. This was unlikely, because the tickets had to be bespoken well in advance. But it was worth checking.

However, when they got there, they could find no trace of the phaeton nor the runaways. Margarethe's extreme fairness was unusual. She was easy to describe and remember. The ostlers shook their heads and the innkeeper couldn't help them.

"I'm run off me feet from morning to night," he said. "I don't remember such a one as you describe. That don't mean she weren't here, mind."

"I'm going on to Barnet," said Trixie decisively, as if daring the Baron to object to that, as well as her other behavior. "It looks as if they went straight up there. As I said, Chauncey wouldn't be able to drive at more than a trot and I think the horses could make it, even though they'd come more or less straight from Tattersall's. It's only about another hour."

"Very well," replied her companion, but said no more.

To tell the truth, he didn't know how to deal with Lady Beatrix Shelby. He had never met a woman like her. The damsels he had known back home were highly sheltered and never allowed to speak to any man outside the family without a chaperone. He had never had any protracted conversation with any of them, much less a conversation like the one he had had with Lady Beatrix. And the women he had known during his time in the army were of a different type altogether. It was not for conversation that one sought their company.

This laughing female with such decided views and complete independence of spirit both shocked and amazed him. She did not wait for him to talk to the ostlers and innkeeper: she had boldly approached them, not looking to see if he were there or not. Inclined to snigger and nudge each other at first, the ostlers soon stood up straight and answered politely. For Beatrix, with all her seeming nonchalance, was unquestionably a lady. She had an air of consequence.

Nevertheless, he knew he was right. Young women needed to be protected, both from the consequence of their own folly and from the lures of men who would mislead them and not give it a second thought. Even Lady Beatrix, for all her independence, would not be immune from the condemnation of society should she make a misstep.

They traveled on to Barnet, where the news was slightly more encouraging. Yes, one of the lads had seen a high perch phaeton. Young feller it were. No, he didn't change his horses; it looked like he was going on to Hatfield.

"Then Hatfield it is," declared Trixie, as she climbed back into the curricle. "He will be obliged to change horses there since he doesn't appear to have done so before."

It took them over an hour to get to Hatfield, because Trixie, having sprung the horses earlier on, was loth to tire them now. Besides, she fully expected at any minute to see Chauncey's phaeton. She was convinced she was close behind him and was surprised not to have overtaken him already. She hadn't thought him such a horseman as to be able to come all this way without mishap.

It was early evening by the time they drew into the small town and the forecourt of the well-known staging inn called *The Eight Bells*, a long, low building fronting onto the main thoroughfare. The late autumn sun was just slipping below the horizon.

Stories abounded that it had been frequented by the infamous highwayman Dick Turpin over seventy-five years before. Unfortunately, it had also become known more recently as the place where a lady traveler's pet dog had been trampled to death by a young blood competing in a curricle race. He had driven his team at top speed onto the forecourt of the inn, causing men and beasts to scatter and the lady's dog to meet its untimely end.

The public outcry had been great, not only against the young man for his flagrant disregard for the safety of others, but also against the inn itself, which was known to profit from its name being associated with contests of this kind. The crowd of mostly well-off young men who routinely bet on such events would spend freely awaiting the outcome of the race and after it.

The lady in question had at length been mollified by a fairly large sum of money and the promise of a new dog. But as a safety measure, the innkeeper had embedded a number of two-foot upright wooden poles along the perimeter of the forecourt, so that carriages could no longer mount the flagstones.

As Trixie and Lukas arrived, it was just that time of day when shadowy remains of light hung in the sky. The earth was dark, but the torches had not yet been lit. Neither of them saw the embedded poles, which under those conditions were indistinguishable from the earth in which they stood. The innkeeper had not thought to paint them white.

Trixie drew up the carriage as she thought parallel to the forecourt but which was, in fact, on a line with the poles. The horses saw them, of course, and avoided them by veering to the left. The side of the curricle came into direct contact with the first stout upright timber, then, as the vehicle was still moving, with a second. There was a sound of splintering wood and the curricle slumped to one side as the wheel broke.

Chapter Nineteen

Trixie was aware of being pitched towards the edge of the seat and knew she could not help but fall. But almost immediately she felt an arm like iron encircle her and hold her fast against what she recognized as the coarse wool of Lukas' cloak. A jolt ran through her, not from fear of falling, but at the sensation of being held so tightly against his chest. She breathed in the manly smell of him.

Rudely awakened from a pleasurable dream in which she was holding five horsemen off from her beloved master by dint of growling so fiercely they all turned and fled, Juno gave a bark and sprang down to see what had happened. She knew nothing of coach wheels but she could tell from the fuss the horses were making that all was not well. In her opinion horses were the most stupid of creatures and the easiest to upset. She had no time for them at all and barked to tell them so. Her bark brought Trixie to her senses. She lifted her head and looked into Lukas' face. He released her. It was hard to read his expression in the semi-dark.

"I beg your pardon, Lady Beatrix," he said in a low voice. "I acted out of instinct, fearing you were about to tumble from the curricle."

"I was, so thank you," she managed to say. "I'm still not sure what happened."

"You ran over some damn fool posts in the ground. They were invisible at this time of the day. Anyone would have done the same. Excuse me, if you are recovered from the shock, I must see to the horses."

Without waiting for a response, Lukas leaped down and went immediately to the bays' heads. Ostlers ran forward to help unhitch them, and other travelers came forward, shaking their heads and opining that the wheel was done for. It was beyond mending. A new one would have to be made.

Trixie got down and had to stand for a moment holding onto the side of the curricle to gain control of her shaking legs. She could now see the posts she had run into. Two of them had been knocked askew. Why on earth hadn't whoever put them up made them taller and painted them white?

When she saw that everything was being done that could be done, she went into the inn, her legs still far from steady, to ask for Mr. Chauncey Shelby. She was certain he must be there. He had not changed horses anywhere and they would not be able to go further. Besides, he would surely not have driven into the night.

The innkeeper met her question distractedly, peering over her shoulder out into the yard where the disturbance was, if anything, increasing. She repeated the name. "There's no one by that name here," he said, finally.

"Come, come," replied Trixie, putting on an air she was far from feeling, "I am Lady Beatrix Shelby. There's no need to hide the truth. I mean him no harm. A youngish man, traveling in a high-perch phaeton with a, er... very fair companion."

"No, my lady. Sorry to disappoint you, but I've never heard of nor seen either of them. There was a young man come through earlier in a high-perch, like you say, but he was alone. He was visiting friends in the neighborhood seemingly, and only stopped to ask their direction."

Trixie was still in shock from the accident and this came as another blow.

"I'm sorry," she said. "I need to sit down for a moment." She went to a bench against the wall. "Why on earth did someone put those posts there like that? I couldn't see them at all. I only hope my bays' hocks have been spared."

She put her head in her hands.

Wringing his hands, the innkeeper explained the reason for the posts. He couldn't decide whether to hover over this lady, who was clearly in distress, or go and see the damage for himself. Finally, he called for a brandy, and when it came, urged Trixie to drink it, before almost running outside.

Trixie took a sip of the fiery liquid and did in fact feel much better. She sat a few more minutes, then went outside and saw the bays being led to the stables, Lukas with them and Juno by his side. When he saw her emerge from the inn, Lukas said something to the dog, who left him and went over to meet Trixie. With Juno sticking to her like glue, she walked over to the tilted curricle and ruefully examined the damage.

A number of men were standing round and a couple of them would have approached her, but Juno gave her low growl the minute anyone gave the impression of coming near. Trixie put her hand on the dog's head.

"It's all right, Juno," she said softly, then said aloud, "Does anyone know where a wheelwright might be found?"

"Thomas Jenkins is a wainwright, Miss," came the answer. "I reckon he can fix that wheel an' all. But I'm thinkin' he's shut up for the night."

She turned towards the person who had spoken, a lad of about fourteen who, now that the torches had been lit, she could see had a shock of red hair. "Would you go and find him? I'll pay for the service."

He turned and ran off. Trixie stood, thinking how she was going to explain this to her uncle, and then wondering what on earth could have happened to Chauncey.

Then it struck her. She and the Baron were obviously not going to be able to make it back to London that night. She had been so sure they would overtake Chauncey, she had not even considered the consequences if they did not, or the impropriety of traveling alone with a man in the dark! She had assumed Margarethe would drive back with her, and Chauncey with the Baron. But this was worse. Far worse! Unless she could find an alternative, they would have to stay overnight in the same inn! Alone with a male companion with no maid, no luggage! My God! It would look to any outside observer that *they* were… she didn't like to even think of the words that described what they could be doing! She could not stay at the inn! What could she do?

She turned to the people around her. "Is there perhaps a widow lady who would take me in overnight? Do you know of one?"

They looked at each other then looked down and shuffled their feet. They knew of no respectable widow who would take in a lady wearing no wedding ring who had arrived alone in the dark with a man. She seemed proper enough, and obviously had a bit of money, but for all that, she was probably no better than she should be. You heard stories about the carryings-on amongst the Quality. It would curl your hair, if everything you heard was true!

When no answer was forthcoming and one would look her in the eye, she guessed what they were thinking. Luckily it was too dark for them to see her blushes. At that moment, the lad came back with a stocky man in a leather apron. He looked her up and down in such a way that she knew he had been apprised of her circumstances.

"Here's for your trouble," she said, giving the lad a coin, and then turned to the man. "You must be the wainwright," she said in her most stately manner, "you can see the state our wheel is in. Are you able to mend it?"

"Aye, I reckon," he said.

"Immediately?"

"Nay," he said at once. "I can't work in the dark, and anyways, I done a full day's work already. I was on the way to me bed when the lad came. And I got to be off early tomorrer. I've got a big job for one of the farmers. Repairin' his wains. He's been waiting nigh on a fortnight to get the rest of his harvest in. Might see me way to doin' it the day after, if I gets finished wiv 'im."

"But surely, if he's been waiting so long already…."

"Nay, Miss. He's got to get it in before the weather changes again. He's already lost a good bit. Him and his beasts'll starve over the winter if he don't finish the harvest, and right quick."

Lukas had returned by now and heard the exchange.

"What the man says is right, Lady Beatrix," he said. "We cannot put our misfortune ahead of the farmer's livelihood. If we have to wait, then we shall. What I can do is to volunteer to help him tomorrow so he can be done all the quicker."

Turning to the wainwright he said, "Tell me where to meet you and when. I'll be there."

"But you're Quality!" said the wainwright with a short laugh. "You don't know about working with your hands!"

"I assure you, I'm no stranger to working with my hands. I haven't been sitting in a parlor drinking port these last few years, nor astride my horse looking down at the men doing the work, like some."

"In the army, were you, sir?" The wainwright looked at him with new respect. "Well, then, if you can lend a hand, I'd be mighty grateful."

Then he held out his hand. "Thomas Jenkins," he said.

"Luke Chorley," said Lukas, shaking it.

"I got to come this way, so I'll pick you up in the cart soon as it's light. 'Bout half past seven that'll be."

"I'll be ready."

The wainwright gave him a sort of salute, and left.

Chapter Twenty

With Juno trotting between them, Lukas walked Trixie away from the crowd that had been listening with all ears to the exchange with the wainwright.

"You will forgive me for calling you Beatrix," said Lukas, as soon as they were out of earshot. "I asked the ostlers if there was another inn and they said there is, but it's out of action due to a fire a couple of months ago. I'm afraid we shall both have to stay here. It's best you be my sister. And the less interested in you I appear to be, the better. That's why I volunteered to go with the wainwright. It's hardly likely a couple bent on a clandestine affair of some sort would be happy to be separated all day."

"So you came to the same conclusions I did!" responded Trixie. "I tried to find a widow to take me in, but no one offered a name. I'm not surprised. I must present an odd appearance. Thank you for acting so swiftly! But if I'm to be your sister, you'd best call me Trixie, everyone close to me does." Then she gasped and put her hand to her mouth. "But I told the innkeeper I was Lady Beatrix Shelby and you just gave your name as Luke Chorley."

Lukas frowned. "Pity. Never mind. You will have to be my half-sister. These people will believe what we tell them, especially if we seem not to be too friendly with each other." He smiled ironically. "That shouldn't be difficult."

She gave a small smile and then said, "Where did *Chorley* come from? Or did you just make it up?"

"My grandfather's name."

"Oh." Then Trixie gave another gasp. "But we're forgetting all about Chauncey and Margarethe! Whatever can become of them?"

"I've been thinking about that," he said, "and I'm afraid we may both have accepted too easily your cousin's assertion that they eloped. We were both too angry to think clearly. I feel responsible for that. I should not have attacked you as I did. I'm sorry. My temper has always been my besetting sin."

He looked ruefully down at her.

"Anyway, wherever they may have gone, it's my belief they never came this way. If they had, they must surely have been observed. A young man barely in control of his phaeton and a very blond pretty young woman, they would stand out! But no one has been able to give us a single report of them. In any case, there is nothing we can do about it now. Our own unfortunate position is more important at the moment."

"Yes," said Trixie, "but you cannot take the whole responsibility for it. You're right. My anger prevented me from thinking clearly before setting off after them, too."

"Perhaps, but *I* should have acted with more forethought."

As Trixie stiffened, he added, "I know your sentiments on the equality of the sexes in respect of the possession of good sense, but we will not argue about it now. You will admit, I hope, that having made your name known to the innkeeper was not the most sensible action. I must now ask you to follow my lead, however much it may go against the grain with you to do so."

After a hesitation, Trixie nodded. Lukas put her arm under his and guided her into the inn. Juno followed.

"Having suffered an unfortunate accident on your doorstep," he announced to the innkeeper in a voice that brooked no dispute, "my sister and I require rooms for the night."

The innkeeper began wringing his hands again. "But we have only one room free, sir. And I'm sorry, but we don't accommodate dogs. Lapdogs, is all right, but a big animal like that…."

Trixie drew in her breath as if to speak, but Lukas squeezed her arm and replied calmly, "My sister will take the room and the dog will stay with her. She is of a nervous disposition and the lack of her maid has already overset her. The dog gives her a sense of security. She is perfectly well behaved. You will put me in with some other gentleman. I shall be away early in the morning, in any case. You may have heard I shall be assisting the wainwright."

The landlord had heard, and looking at Trixie, whose gaze was fixed on the floor, thought she did indeed look the type to have the vapors. Up in the boughs one minute down in the ditch the next. It was easier to do as this haughty gentleman wished. Besides they both looked as if they could pay for it. So if he had objections to a large dog staying in one of his best rooms, he made no comment. Instead, he nodded and said, "I daresay the young man in the front room will agree to share with you, if it means you will also share the cost."

"Certainly. And we shall require dinner for ourselves and also this animal. She may eat in the kitchen, but I shall make sure she is fed properly. I do not want any chicken bones sticking in her throat."

The landlord didn't know what his wife would say when told not only that a large dog would be in one of her best bedchambers, but she was also to feed it in her kitchen and be supervised doing so. But he knew she would agree on the subject of money, so he changed the subject, saying only, "I'm afraid there's no private parlor available, if that's what her ladyship was wanting."

So he had remembered her name, thought Trixie ruefully. But Lukas replied calmly, "We do not require a private parlor. The public room will be quite satisfactory so long as no one smokes in there. My sister becomes ill at the scent of tobacco."

"Oh no, sir, my wife forbids smoking in the parlor. The smell gets in everything, she says. Gentlemen 'ave to go into the taproom or outside if they wishes to smoke."

He may be dreadfully strict and old-fashioned, Trixie said to herself, *but he is good at taking command. And no one could imagine us a romantic couple, the way he has described me!*

The landlord called for a maid to show Trixie to her room and bustled away to arrange the lodging for Lukas. Meanwhile, Lukas took Juno to the kitchen, where he smiled at the innkeeper's wife so charmingly that in spite of her husband's misgivings, she said afterwards she would have fed a dozen dogs to get such a handsome man to smile at her again.

He stayed there while Juno ate and then took the dog outside. She ran around on her own business while Lukas washed his hands and face under the pump. They came in just as Trixie was descending the stairs. Juno greeted her joyously with a whine, a whip of her tail and by bumping her nose under her hand for a snout rub.

"It's very strange," Lukas remarked quietly. "As a rule she goes to no one. But she seems much taken with you."

Unlike her master then, thought Trixie, but said nothing as they walked into the parlor dining room with Juno close to her skirts. The other diners took little notice. This was the country, after all. Dogs were not uncommon, though this one was a little larger than usual. Juno settled by Trixie's feet, a good instinct, it subsequently proved, as she surreptitiously fed her tidbits from the table. *I knew I liked this one,* she thought.

The meal was not very refined, but it was copious, and they were both hungry. Their quiet conversation was limited to running over the accident again, and the unknown whereabouts of the pair they were chasing. But once they had finished, Lukas said in a voice loud enough for the other diners to hear, "No, Trixie, I refuse to allow you to go there."

Juno looked up, but obviously decided there was nothing amiss, for she settled her head down again. Trixie, however, was taken aback until she looked at Lukas and found he had a meaningful look in his eye. She understood. "But brother," she said, in a whining voice, "I most particularly desire to see my old friend."

"Her brother, you mean," he replied. "I've told you before I shall never agree to that match."

"But he's such a good man. He hopes to be named curate to the parish."

"If you think I shall allow you to become engaged to a would-be curate, you are much mistaken. Have you no family pride?"

"Oh brother! I would not believe anyone could be so cruel!" cried Trixie, standing up. "I'm going to my room!"

With that, she ran out of the room, leaving all listeners with the exact impression Lukas had intended: that brother and sister did not see eye to eye. Juno, after a nod from him, went after her.

In fact, Trixie was glad to retire. She was tired after her long day of driving. Her arms and shoulders were aching, and an enforced day of rest was not an unwelcome prospect. She removed her creased clothing and looked at it critically. It all needed a good brushing. And the bed felt as if it might be damp. How she missed her maid! Alice would have put in a hot brick long since, and would have taken away her mistress's clothing to perform some magic to restore it.

She felt all too acutely how stupid she had been to take off after Chauncey on the basis of nothing but Mariah's suspicions. Lukas was right. Mariah's head was full of romantic nonsense. Did that mean Margarethe's was too, and if so, was it truly her fault, as her brother thought, because she had given them those silly books to read? Then she thought about that invented dispute with Lukas. Did he really consider her to have no pride? Had those words spoken in a form of play-acting revealed his true opinion of her? She told herself she didn't care what his opinion of her was, but she knew she was lying. She remembered the jolt that had gone through her when he took hold of her. Even thinking about it now made her shiver. And his handling of the situation had been masterful. What could have been a scene of intense embarrassment had been avoided thanks to his quick thinking.

She sighed, patted Juno on the head and climbed into bed in her chemise. It wasn't really damp, just chilly. But the feather mattress was comfortable, the blankets heavy and warm. Her room was on the back of the inn and it was quiet. She soon fell asleep, hearing neither the ostlers shouting to each other at the end of their day of work, nor the mice scratching in the wainscotting. Juno heard all of it, but decided nothing constituted a threat to this person she knew she had to protect. Soon, she too, was asleep.

Lukas stayed in the dining parlor another hour and then made his way upstairs. His roommate proved to be a mild-looking solicitor's clerk who was rather stunned when the tall, broad-shouldered man with military bearing came into the room. But they shook hands and each prepared for bed. The clerk extracted a nightshirt and cap from a capacious bag and climbed into a big bed that squeaked when he moved.

Like Trixie, Lukas had nothing but what he stood up in, and like her, too, he missed having a servant who would clean his boots and brush his clothes. But then, he thought, after a day working with the wainwright in a farm yard they would be worse before they got better. He stripped down to his drawers, surreptitiously took his money roll and pistol out of his cloak pockets and put them under his pillow. He spread the cloak itself on the truckle bed put up for him. It was not as comfortable as Trixie's bed, but like the soldier he was, he soon fell asleep. He'd slept in worse. Much worse.

Chapter Twenty-One

His experience in the army had accustomed Lukas to waking at dawn, so he was downstairs and waiting for the wainwright when he showed up in a creaking cart loaded with the tools of his trade. He had used his influence with the innkeeper's wife to have coffee and bread and cheese ready for him, the one in a metal can and the other wrapped in a piece of cloth. He offered to share both with the wainwright, who declined, saying his wife had given him something before he left.

"You married, sir?" he asked.

"No," said Lukas, munching his bread and cheese. "Neither the opportunity nor the inclination."

"The opportunity I can understand, you being in the army, an' all," said the other man, "but the inclination, that's another thing. Any man's got to want his own wife, keeping the fire burning, having his meal ready, keep him warm at night, if yer knows what I mean. Not to mention the young 'uns."

"Perhaps you're right, but I've never yet met a woman I was prepared to spend my life with, even with the advantages you mention."

Even as he said it, Lukas wondered why that was. Did he have impossibly high standards? What would he look for in a wife, after all? He pondered on this a while, and came to the conclusion he wanted a woman he could talk to. He'd like her to be comely, or at least, not downright bracket-faced, but most of all, he wanted to be able to discuss things with her. Then he thought about Beatrix. She was more than comely, and the conversation he'd had with her was the longest he'd ever had with any woman except his mother. It was a shame her views were so contrary to his own, for he had to admit, she was in other respects almost perfect. But he pitied the man she married.

The wainwright broke into his thoughts. "Here we are, sir. Peckett's Farm. I've got to repair both haywains back there in the barn. Lookee," he handed Lukas a homespun smock and leather apron like the ones he was wearing. "You'd best take off that fine coat and shirt you've got on there, sir. Put these on. Bad enough you've got t' wear them good boots, but nothing I've got would fit your size, I don't reckon."

Lukas looked at his feet. "Yes, I've got big feet, no gainsaying it. The bootmaker charges me extra!"

"Big feet mean a big prick, so they say, sir. All the more reason for gettin' yerself a wife!"

They both laughed, as men will whenever the masculine equipment is mentioned. That sealed their friendship and they set to work together. Lukas knew nothing of cart or wheel making, but he was willing to learn, and did whatever the wainwright asked. He was set at first to the mundane chores like doing the first rough cuts, while the wainwright did the cutting and shaping. Later he was permitted to use sandpaper to sand down the pieces.

They worked companionably till the church clock rang noon, when Thomas stood up and said, "Time fer a bite, I reckon."

His wife had sent two huge wedges of pigeon pie, and the farmer's wife brought them over an enamel ewer of beer with two mugs. Sitting in the shade of a huge chestnut tree, Lukas thought nothing had ever tasted so delicious, nor had the setting ever been more perfect. His back against the trunk of the tree, he could see over the gently undulating landscape of Hertfordshire, the autumn fields a patchwork of brown and yellow.

By five in the afternoon they were packing up the wainwright's cart and saying farewell to the farmer, who counted eleven shillings carefully into Thomas's hand, before bidding him and Lukas a thankful goodbye.

As they trotted down the lane back towards the inn, Thomas said, "You've earned a good day's wage, Luke," (for by now they were both on first name terms and the Baron had used the anglicized version of his name) "and no mistake. Six pence is what I'd pay an apprentice, and I'd be glad to give you double that. You earned it."

He reached into his pocket and handed Lukas a shilling.

Lukas took it, then pressed it back into his palm. "You buy that wife of yours a trinket from me. That was the best pie I ever ate, so mind you do! Besides, what I learned today is worth more than a shilling. You watch, Thomas! I'll set myself up in competition with you! I'm almost tempted to repair that wheel of mine myself!"

Thomas thought it a very good joke, and repeated it later to his wife, while taking the shilling and putting it in a vase they kept on the mantle. It was a hideous thing, but it had come down to Thomas from his mother, who had it from hers, so it kept pride of place in their tiny parlor. The wainwright's wife would take it out the following summer when the fair came to town, and spend a delicious Sunday afternoon buying a comb for her hair, a hoop for her son, and ribbons for her daughters.

Promising to be back the next day to repair the wheel, Thomas dropped Lukas off at *The Eight Bells*.

"Keep the smock and apron if yer want to help tomorrer," he said.

Lukas said he would, and went around the corner to the pump to wash off the dust of the day.

Trixie had slept late, until Juno nudged her awake with the obvious message that she needed to go out. She scrambled into her clothes, pulled on her stockings and boots, and attempted to tame her curls. Not having been confined in a nightcap, they now burst unmanageably from her head. Giving up the attempt to put her bonnet on the wild mass, she went downstairs, with Juno close behind her. It was a lovely morning, the autumnal mist burning off to reveal a blue sky and leave the air crisp and dry.

She walked around to the stables to check on her uncle's bays, who seemed none the worse for wear. They nickered when they saw her, and she patted their velvety muzzles, promising to come back later with apples or carrots, if she could get some.

Juno found her in the stables, where she demonstrated her scorn for horses by ignoring them altogether. Going back inside, Beatrix asked for tea and bread and butter to be brought up to her room. This arrived with a cheerful, apple-cheeked maid who called Juno a good old lady and was allowed to pat her. Encouraged by Juno's friendliness, Trixie asked the girl if it would be possible for her to have a bath once the morning rush was over, and if someone would be able to brush her riding clothes. And a hairbrush would be most welcome.

It took a little while, but later in the morning, a lad arrived with a tin hipbath, which he dumped in the room before backing away, his eye on a growling Juno. He was followed by two maids, each with two ewers of hot water. From somewhere they had found a sliver of sweet-smelling soap, which was more than Trixie had hoped for. She divested herself of her outer clothing and handed it to the maids for brushing.

When they were gone, she removed her petticoat, stockings and chemise and stepped into the bath, which had a tall sloping back and a shallow basin, too short for her to sit down in unless she held her legs close to her chest. Nevertheless, the warm water was delicious. She soaped herself all over and then, in order to rinse herself, had to slide down and put her legs over the end of the tub onto the floor. When she stood up, Juno, who had been lying off to the side, looked up but clearly found her naked state totally uninteresting.

Trixie quickly dried herself and put on her underclothing. She got back into bed to keep warm while awaiting the arrival of her clothes, which came a short time later. The maids refilled the ewers with the by now cool and scummy water and put the tub outside. As they were leaving, one of them put her hand in her apron pocket and pulled out a hairbrush. "This is mine, Miss, if you'd like to use it. It's clean, no nits or nothing like that. I'm partic'lar that way."

"Thank you both very much," said Trixie, and reached for her reticule.

From the small sum of money she had with her, she gave them each a silver coin, which they took as if they'd never had a sixpence to spend before, which perhaps they hadn't. They earned ten pounds a year, most of which was sent home. They both had numerous brothers and sisters to help support and rarely had anything for themselves. They both bobbed a curtsey and left, talking excitedly together.

She brushed her hair and put it in a braid down her back, which was all she could manage. She laughed at herself in the small mirror. Thank goodness none of her smart friends could see her! Then, feeling very much better, she went downstairs for a late luncheon. Juno knew the trick by now and lay quietly by her feet, graciously receiving pieces of ham and cheese.

Chapter Twenty-Two

Trixie went up to her bed after lunch, and lay there, telling herself she was not missing Lukas. She kept coming back to the intense sensation his strong arms had given her. She had never been held like that before. The young men who fancied themselves in love with her had tried to embrace her, of course, but she had always been able to escape their arms with no difficulty. That iron-like clasp she had felt yesterday would have been impossible to get out of, even had she wanted to. She fell asleep wondering what Lukas was doing and when he would be back.

Later in the afternoon, determined to shake off her mood, she took Juno for a walk over the fields behind the inn. They wandered through an orchard, where a few late apples lay on the ground. She had to flap away the wasps, but she managed to pick up a few and put them in her cloak pockets.

By the time they arrived back at the inn, unknown to Trixie, Lukas had been dropped off and was at the pump. She strolled carelessly around the side of the building, meaning to take the promised apples to the bays. Then she stopped dead in her tracks.

Naked to the waist, Lukas had just lifted his broad shoulders from under the pump. He shook his head like a dog, and drops of water flew out, sparkling in the late afternoon sun. Its rays lit up the muscles in his chest and back and along his arms. The hair on his chest was wet and lay dark against his skin. He picked up a towel that lay a couple of feet away, and began to rub himself vigorously. He didn't notice her standing there until Juno gave a short bark and ran towards him. Then he turned and stared at Trixie, as she stared at him.

Lukas was the first to recover. He threw the towel to the ground and reached for his shirt, which Trixie now saw was folded neatly on one side. He pulled it over his head. He ran his fingers through his hair, which, in its uncombed state, waved slightly. He picked up his other clothing on the cobbles and came towards her. Trixie tried to speak, but no words came.

"It was hot and dusty work," he said apologetically. "A soldier's habit, I'm afraid. See a pump. Use it."

"O... of course. I took a bath myself." She found her voice, and to her dismay, began to gabble. "After breakfast. It was very pleasant. The maids even gave me some scented soap. And a hairbrush. Not that I could do much with my hair. I'm quite hopeless without my maid."

She finally ran down. Lukas stared at her. He had noticed her hair, in fact. She usually wore it in complicated curls on the top of her head, but now it was in a simple thick braid down her back, with curling tendrils escaping here and there. He thought she looked very pretty. Less the Lady Beatrix and more the Trixie.

"I like it like that," he said. "It's how the unmarried girls wear it back home."

"And yours is quite wavy," Trixie blurted out, before she could stop herself.

What was the matter with her? She knew one simply did not make personal remarks like this to a gentleman. She'd known Corny forever, and she wouldn't dream of talking about his hair.

She took a deep beath. "Anyway," she said. "I must go. I've got some apples for the bays. I promised them."

He smiled. It was a lovely smile and her heart lurched. "And one must always keep one's promises," he said.

He bowed and walked off. Juno looked at him, then at her.

"Go on, then," she said. "I know you love him."

Juno trotted after her master, leaving Trixie feeling as if her life were like a kaleidoscope, where the pieces had just been rearranged into a different picture: her life before the vision at the pump, and her life after it.

Her mind elsewhere, Trixie fed the bays their apples, and only came to the present when the head groom approached her.

"Them bays is fine animals," he said. "Mr. Luke has told us what he wants doin'," he said. "He knows his horses. 'Course, he was in the cavalry, so no surprise there."

Trixie hadn't known that. In fact, she realized she knew very little about him at all. But she could not stop herself from dwelling on the image of Lukas as he stood up from the pump. Then she shook herself and made a decision. She asked the innkeeper for a piece of paper and a pen or pencil. He searched around and came up with a scrap of paper and a chewed pencil.

"It's the best I can do, my lady," he said. "It's not a thing I often gets asked for."

She thought for a few minutes and then swiftly wrote.

"Please take this note up to M... my brother," she said. "And kindly have a meal sent to my room later. I shall not be dining downstairs this evening."

When Lukas received her note a few minutes later, he read it, then thoughtfully folded it and put it in his pocket.

Dear Baron,

 Please excuse me for not dining with you this evening. Like the poor woman you made me out to be,

> *I always sleep poorly when I'm from home, and I find I am very tired. I hope the wheel may be repaired tomorrow, so that we may leave. I am anxious to get home, as I am sure you are, too.*
> *Beatrix Shelby*

It was not true that Trixie was tired. In fact she was well rested. But her mind was in turmoil. She simply could not face him over the dinner table and make light conversation. Her evening meal arrived in due course. She ate it without appetite and then undressed for bed. She lay awake a long time, and that night, she did indeed sleep poorly.

Chapter Twenty-Three

Downstairs, Lukas took Juno to the kitchens for her dinner, and then went upstairs for his own. He ate everything put in front of him. Again, it was not particularly good, but he had been too often hungry to refuse food when it was offered. Juno lay at his feet and received the tidbits that came her way with enthusiasm. "I'm glad you're enjoying it, at any rate," he said to the dog. "You'll be as spoiled as any overfed pug if this continues."

Juno thumped her long tail. She liked the sound of that.

They went out for a stroll afterwards, Lukas wishing he had a cigar, which was his only self-indulgence. But he was tired after the early start and hard work of the day, and it wasn't long before he, too, went to bed. The wainwright would be there at first light to repair the curricle wheel, hoping to get the job done by noon. The clerk had moved on and the room was his. He used the wide bed and, unlike Trixie, for the first time in a long while, slept the night through with Juno by his side.

When Trixie stepped outside the next day around mid-morning, it took her a moment to recognize the Baron. He had put the smock and leather apron back on and was bent over next to the wainwright for all the world like a man born to the work. It was only his blond head that distinguished him. Her heart beat fiercely and she felt too shy to approach him. She simply watched until Juno saw her and trotted over to wish her good day.

She patted the dog's head. "I'm going for a walk," she said. "I recommend you come with me. We'll be a long time in the curricle later on."

She was both excited by the prospect of those hours in the curricle, and dreading them. She had tried simply waiting in the parlor, but found herself too keyed up. Now she and Juno walked the way they had gone the day before, collecting a few more apples. By the time they came back, the wheel was affixed to the curricle, the wainwright had gone and Lukas was nowhere in sight. She peeped around the side of the building, but the pump was standing innocently alone. She didn't know whether she was glad or sorry as she continued to the stables to give the apples to the bays.

As she went back into the inn, Lukas was coming down the stairs, carrying a bundle. He was dressed as a gentleman once more, his coat brushed and his boots clean. He looked very handsome.

"Lad… Trixie!" he said. "There you are. I'm glad you didn't wander off. The wheel is repaired. We fixed it up quite quickly in the end. Go into the parlor. I've asked them to bring luncheon at once. We should get on the road as soon as possible." he indicated the bundle in his hands. "I just need to take this to the scullery for washing. It's the smock the wainwright lent me."

Trixie felt as if a pail of water had been thrown in her face. *I'm glad you didn't wander off. Go into the parlor. We should get on the road.* No *if you please, if you agree, would you like…*. He was treating her exactly as if she really were his sister, and a silly one, at that! She was infuriated to feel tears coming to her eyes. She dashed them away angrily as she stalked into the parlor and sat down. Yes, by all means let them get on the road as soon as possible, let them get back to London as soon as possible, let her be rid of this rude, overbearing man as soon as possible! She drew in a deep breath and set her chin. Enough of this foolishness! She was Lady Beatrix Shelby, a favorite of the Prince Regent, courted by gentlemen all over London. She didn't need the Baron Lukas von Schwerin!

Luncheon was consumed in almost total silence. Juno was disappointed when Trixie gave her nearly nothing. Then Trixie went up to her room to wash her hands and put on her bonnet. She had redone her hair in a braid, mostly because she was not adept at anything else, but also because Lukas had said he liked it. Now she looked at it and scoffed. *You're a fool, my lady*, she said to her reflection in the mirror, and jammed her bonnet on her head.

"I shall take the reins today," said Lukas, when she met him in front of the inn, Juno at his side.

"Certainly not!" snapped Trixie. "The curricle and the bays belong to my uncle. They are my responsibility."

"But your note yesterday said you sleep poorly when from home. I imagined you must be tired." Lukas was taken aback by her vehemence.

"I know you think we women too foolish to do anything, but I'm not too tired to drive a curricle and pair."

"I've never said that all women are foolish," he answered mildly. "But as you wish. Allow me to help you up."

She would have swatted his hand away, but the strong grip with which he held her arm brought back the sensation of the day of the wheel accident and she couldn't help herself allowing him to hand her up into the vehicle.

He went around to the other side and nimbly leaped up with Juno right behind him. She touched her whip to the leader's ear, and they were off.

Her bad temper had more than one unfortunate consequence. First of all, it made the journey back to London very unpleasant. It was accomplished in almost total silence, with monosyllabic exchanges to discuss if they should stop at Barnet. No, it was agreed on both sides. They preferred to carry on and get home.

But more importantly, as it turned out, Trixie had paid no attention to a carriage that had come to a halt at the other end of the forecourt. But the lady who presently descended certainly paid attention to her.

"Look! Isn't that Trixie Shelby?" she said to her companion. "I'm sure it is. But who's that with her? My word, he's good-looking! But I've never seen him before in my life. Have you?"

"Never," replied her friend. "A man like that would be hard to forget."

"And look at her hair!" said the first. "It's all anyhow! She must have had no maid to arrange it for her. It's almost as if," and her eyes grew round, "she *slept* in it like that!"

"You don't mean...."

"Yes, I do! Let's find out inside if she was here *overnight* with that man."

The two ladies swept into the inn and smiled at the innkeeper.

Tell me, my good man," said the first. "Was that Lady Beatrix Shelby we saw leaving just a moment ago. She was with a blond gentleman...."

"Yes, Madam, Lady Shelby was here with her brother, Mr. Luke Chorley." He did not mention the accident with the wheel. No need to implicate the inn in anything disagreeable. "They stayed here er... unexpectedly."

"Indeed? How interesting. I was not aware she had a brother."

"A half-brother, I believe Madam. A very pleasant gentleman."

"Such a pity! We just missed them! It would have been most agreeable to have a coze over luncheon!"

The two ladies moved away into the parlor dining room. They were also on their way back to London. They had just spent a couple of weeks with a school friend who had married a well-to-do squire and now lived some miles north of Hatfield. The first part of their journey had been spent pitying poor Amelia, buried away in the country with a husband who fell asleep after dinner and snored, and who was sadly putting on flesh.

The second half of the journey would be spent discussing what to do with the delicious gossip about Lady Beatrix Shelby they alone were in possession of. They were in their second season and had watched Trixie, only in her first, sweep all before her. Not that they were jealous, of course, nor did they wish her any ill. There was no doubt a simple and innocent explanation. But she *had* stayed overnight in the inn with a gentleman who had been passed off as her half-brother, when everyone knew she had no brother at all. She *had* been seen being helped into a curricle by that same gentleman with no maid or luggage in sight. And her hair *had* been loosely braided, as if she had just got out of bed, there was no denying it! One wouldn't tell *everyone*, just a few good friends, sworn to secrecy, of course. *Of course.*

Chapter Twenty-Four

Trixie drove the horses as fast as she dared, anxious to be home and be rid of her passenger. The evening was just drawing in when they drew up in front of Uncle Leonard's town house. She had remembered they'd left the Baron's curricle and pair there. How she wished she'd instructed the grooms to drive them home. She decided she would get rid of him anyway. She didn't care what he thought of her manners.

"I shall drive you straight to the mews, Baron," she said. "I'm sure you will wish to go home as soon as possible."

"Of course, Lady Beatrix," he responded, recognizing that all familiarity between them was at an end and knowing she was anxious for him to be gone. He had spent best part of the journey wondering what had caused her ladyship's change of demeanor. She had been so friendly the day before, then today she would scarcely look at him. But women were unaccountable creatures, he knew. It was useless to try to analyze their motives.

"Pole up the Baron's pair at once," she said to the grooms who ran forward as soon as they reached the stables. She turned to her passenger. "I'll leave you here. The men will see to you. Goodbye." Juno looked up, surprised at the severity in her voice. She patted her briefly. "Goodbye to you, too, Juno."

And she slipped swiftly to the ground and strode off.

Lukas shrugged, got down with Juno close behind him and went to help with the tired bays.

Trixie pulled the bell of her own front door furiously, scarcely able to restrain her impatience to be inside. When the butler opened the door, she pushed past him, saying "Who's at home, Foljambe?"

"Good afternoon, my lady," replied the butler, whom a lifetime of service had rendered immune to his employers' displays of bad manners, "I believe both Lady Mariah and Lord Chauncey are in the drawing room. The Countess is in her room and Mr. Leonard is in the library."

"Chauncey is *here*?"

"Yes, my lady. He went for a ride earlier, but he returned several hours ago."

Trixie burst into the drawing room, where she discovered her cousins reading, she a *Mode Illustrée* and he the *Sporting Gazette*.

"Trixie!" cried Mariah, leaping up. "Where have you been? We were so worried about you!"

"I was chasing after Chauncey and Margarethe, of course! It was you who said they had eloped!"

"Oh that!" said Chauncey with a laugh. "That was all rot! I went to the park to show the other fellows my phaeton. We all took a nice little ride up to Hampstead. Had a bumper or two and came home."

"He was drunk!" said Mariah with disgust. "If Mama hadn't been so glad to see him she would have given him a tongue lashing. As it was, she fell on his neck and begged his forgiveness. Said of course he could keep the phaeton now that he's a man!"

"Why on earth would you think I'd eloped with Margarethe, anyway?" added Chauncey. "She's like a sister to me! You don't elope with your sister, for God's sake!"

"But where have you *been*, Trixie?" Mariah ran to her cousin. "You've been gone *two days*! You can't have gone all the way to Scotland, surely?"

"Don't be ridiculous! It would take a lot longer than that to get to Scotland!" said her brother. "Didn't that governess teach you anything?"

"We, or rather, I, broke a wheel on the curricle and had to get it mended," said Trixie. "The wheelwright couldn't get to it right away."

"What do you mean *we?*" said Mariah. "You don't mean you were with that awful Baron all the time?"

"Yes, I was, of course I was. I didn't mean to be gone even one day. I made sure we'd find Chauncey and Margarethe in a ditch a few miles up the road, and bring them home."

"Thanks very much!" muttered Chauncey.

Trixie ignored him. "But when we didn't, we went on to Hatfield and had the accident, so we had to stay."

"But Trixie! How could you stay with a *man?*"

"I didn't stay *with* him. We both stayed in the inn, that's all. Besides, we told them he was my brother. There was no problem."

"But did he *pay* for you?" Mariah was insistent.

"I suppose he did, come to think of it. I only had the few shillings in my reticule. He must have paid for the repair of the wheel too. Oh dear! I wish I'd thought of that before! I'll have to pay him back."

She made a face. She had hoped never to see him again.

Foljambe must have sent word to the other members of the household that Lady Trixie was back, for her uncle now came into the room, closely followed by her aunt. The whole story had to be told again.

Her uncle's response was typical of him. "You didn't injure the bays, did you?" he said.

"No, uncle, they were very well taken care of. But the new wheel on the curricle will need to be painted to match the rest. You may go and look in the stables if you don't believe me."

"I think I shall go and take a gander. I must say, Trixie, I wouldn't have thought it of you! Driving into a stationary post! I taught you better than that!"

"You would have driven into it too! It was invisible! And I must say, I find it distressing that none of you seem to care a fig for whether I was injured!"

"Were you?" asked her uncle.

"No." said Trixie sullenly.

"Well then, I shall go and look at my bays." Her uncle left the room, muttering, "I? Drive into stationary posts? Never!"

The Countess, like Mariah, was much more concerned with the proprieties than with the possibility of Trixie having suffered an injury.

"I cannot imagine why you would think my Chauncey would act so improperly. He knows what is owed to his name! It is you and your impetuousness that has led to this grave error, Trixie! Now you arrive home with your hair looking like you have passed the night in a hedge! I hope to God no one saw you and that no one ever hears anything about this! Is that Baron likely to say something, do you think?"

"No, he won't say anything to anyone. He isn't a person who converses at all! He simply gives orders and expects them to be carried out!"

With that, she burst into tears and ran from the room to bury her head in her pillow and weep as if her heart would break.

Chapter Twenty-Five

Lukas drove home his well-rested grays and was greeted with cries of joy by his mother and sister.

"Lukas!" cried his mother. "Thank goodness you're here at last. Where on earth have you been? We came home earlier today and Fritz said you were here with a large dog briefly the day before yesterday but then disappeared! And I see you have brought the dog back again." She tentatively gave Juno a light pat on the head.

"Yes, Mama, this is Juno, Grandfather's old gun dog. She wouldn't stay behind at Chorley House. She's perfectly well behaved."

"We only just saw your letter," added Margarethe, throwing her arms around his neck. "We never would have gone away if we'd known you were coming. And what a sweet old dog!"

She sank to her knees and hugged Juno.

Lukas laughed. "This is the welcome I was hoping for when I arrived the other day. Instead of that, the house was almost empty and I received the most extraordinary intelligence from Fritz."

"Come and sit down and tell us where you've been!" His sister dragged him into the drawing room and sat next to him, holding his hand, her face alight. Juno followed them all and curled up in front of the fire with a sigh.

"I hope you don't mind, Mama," said Lukas, indicating the dog. "I found her curled up just so at Chorley House."

"Of course not. She's a connection to my father. She's welcome here."

But when the ladies heard where he had gone and why, they looked at him in dismay.

"You mean you actually believed I'd *eloped*, and with *Chauncey*?" cried Margarethe. "Oh Lukas, how could you think that of me?"

Tears came to her eyes, and she buried her face in her hands.

"I'm sorry, Grete," he said, putting his arm around her and using the diminutive she'd invented for herself when she was little, "Of course, I realize now I must have been mad! But it was those two women! They were so bold and sure of themselves and… well, you said in your letter Beatrix was your friend, so I thought…."

"So Trixie believed it too?" Margarethe was horrified.

"Yes, though it was that cousin of hers, Mariah, who suggested it. But she seemed to think it likely enough and proposed going after you — to save Chauncey, mark you! What could I do but go with her?"

"Oh, Mama!" Margarethe threw Lukas's arm from her shoulders and ran to her mother. She sank down in front of her and put her head in her lap. "Do you think I have such a bad reputation, now, that anyone would believe such a thing?"

"Of course not, my dear! Don't be in such a taking! If anyone's reputation may be ruined, it's Lady Beatrix's. She spent the night at an inn with your brother."

Margarethe looked with round eyes at Lukas. "So she did!"

"But we made sure no one thought anything of it," said Lukas, quickly. "We pretended she was my sister. Even had an argument in the parlor to prove it!"

"Your sister!"

"Yes, God forbid! If she were my sister I think I would have to lock her in a tower like in those books of yours!"

"Oh, Lady Beatrix is not a bad girl," said the Baroness. "A little wild, that's all. She needs a strong husband to steady her. And she would make a good wife: she has a heart of gold. She's done everything she could to bring Margarethe out of herself. You know how shy you've always been, my dear. And she's very loyal. Lukas, you said yourself she wanted to save her cousin Chauncey. It's not everyone who would chase after a here-and-thereian like him."

"Hmm," said Lukas. He was thinking of the heated conversation he had with her, and of her set face and silent demeanor on the way home. He simply didn't understand her. But Juno loved her. It was odd, but that was decidedly in her favor.

"Nevertheless, I think I shall not be so close a friend as I have been," declared Margarethe, "I shall write her a letter."

"I shouldn't, my dear," said her mother. "Let things die down for a day or two."

"No, Mama, I wish her to know my feelings. I am most upset."

She stood up and walked firmly out of the room.

"Oh dear!" said her Mama. "I hope she doesn't burn her bridges. As I say, I see no harm in Beatrix. In fact, I hoped Margarethe would have a steadying influence on her. Now, Lukas, my love, let me tell you my news and why we have been away."

Chapter Twenty-Six

Trixie had a disturbed night in which she dreamed of broken carriage wheels, braids coming undone and half-naked men with rivulets of water running down their bodies. She awoke very little rested, and looked so hollow eyed, her governess urged her to stay in bed.

"For it stands to reason, my love, you have had a long and wasted journey and your spirits are quite overset. I shall bring you a tisane and some little cakes. That will make you feel better."

This had been her infallible remedy when Trixie was growing up, and it certainly suited her now, when she was feeling more low than she could ever remember being in her life.

Things were not improved when towards midday she received a letter from Margarethe von Schwerin.

Dear Lady Beatrix,

My brother has told me how you and he went on a wild goose chase, thinking I had eloped with your cousin. I'm sorry you wasted your time and met with an accident besides. But I am even more unhappy, and, frankly, insulted, that you should both have thought so ill of me as to believe I would do such a thing.

Lukas I am able to forgive, for he has not seen me for many months, and even before that, we were not often together. He was brought up in England, as you know, and then was precipitated into almost constant war for several years.

But you, Lady Beatrix, I thought you had known me better. We have seen each other nearly daily for several months now. We have had intimate discussions. I have reviewed them all and nowhere do I think I have given you reason to consider me of such weak will and low character that I should ever consent to an elopement, much less with the son of a family that has always shown me such kindness.

You have given me novels, and I have read them with enjoyment. We have laughed over them together. But I do not think I have led you to believe I consider them the model of behavior for a gentlewoman. I thought them entertaining but silly, and my mother, with whom I discussed the matter, agreed entirely. Let me tell you plainly: I repudiate absolutely the ideas they contain, especially that of entering into a marriage without the full support of one's parents. I would never elope with anyone!

It will perhaps help if I tell you that the person with whom I left the house three days ago was Arno Witherspoon. He conveyed me to their home in the country, whither my mother had gone the day before. You see, Arno's father has asked my mother to marry him, and she has accepted. She went to see her future home.

She had ordered an evening cloak, but it had not arrived by the day of her departure. She did not want to delay her trip, because the housekeeper had already arranged a tea party with the ladies of local families. I said I would wait and bring it along the next day, and Arno was kind enough to drive me.

Mr. Witherspoon did not want to publish the notice of their betrothal until after Mama had been to Nightingale House (their home), that is why no one knew about it. I am very happy to say the visit was a great success and I'm sure the marriage will be, too. Mr. Witherspoon knew Mama before she married my father; they were young together years ago in London, and have a great deal in common.

I am sure you will understand, Lady Beatrix, when I say it is better if we cease to pursue the close relationship we had before. It is clear to me now that our convictions are far from the same. While I like and admire you, it is obvious we see things very differently.

Please accept my grateful thanks, and that of my mother, for the many kindnesses you have shown us both over the last months,
Yours very sincerely,
Margarethe von Schwerin

Trixie looked up from this missive, her face drained of all color. The shock of the carriage wheel accident was nothing compared with this! The von Schwerins blamed her for everything! Oh, she could hear the voice of the Baron: *I repudiate the ideas they contain, cease to pursue the close relationship, our convictions are far from the same!* She ground her teeth. He had been as ready to believe Mariah as she had! And an engagement between that old fossil Witherspoon and the Baroness? They had certainly kept that a secret. What about Uncle Leonard? What was he going to say?

She flung off the bedcovers and marched furiously up and down. It was too bad! After all her efforts on everyone's behalf! She would have to quietly explain the situation to her uncle. And Corny! He had been showing a decided preference for Margarethe! She would have to warn him how stuffy they all were, especially the Baron! She would hate for him to involve himself with such a family before knowing what he was getting into.

She sat down immediately and wrote him a note:

Dear Corny,

Come to see me as soon as you can. I have something I need to tell you.

Your friend,

Trixie

Then she nibbled the end of her pen and, with a great deal of stopping and starting, composed a note for Margarethe.

Dear Margarethe,

I'm sorry you find it necessary to put an end to our close relationship. I do not believe I err when I perceive the influence of the Baron in this decision. He expressed his disapproval of my opinions during our fruitless trip to Hatfield, a trip which I hope he has admitted he readily undertook, thus proving his judgement no different from my own.

My uncle and I are delighted to hear of your mother's engagement to Mr. Witherspoon. I'm sure their mutual memories will ensure a happy marriage. We both wish them every happiness, a happiness that I hope you also, dear Margarethe, will enjoy in your future life, wherever it may take you.

Yours always in friendship,

Beatrix Shelby

She sealed both notes, rang for her maid and had her take them down for immediate delivery.

"Come back afterwards, Alice," she said. "I am getting dressed. And I must have you do my hair. It has looked a positive fright for three days now."

Chapter Twenty-Seven

Sometime later, Lady Trixie Shelby went looking for her uncle. She looked very modish in a new evening gown of amber silk embellished with ivory lace. Her hair has been brushed till it shone and was piled on top of her head in a complicated arrangement, with loose ringlets dropping prettily over her ears.

She found him in the library, looking at his *sang de boeuf* collection. He looked up as she came in, and his face beamed in pleasure. He had apparently forgotten all about the repaired curricle and his bays.

"You're up!" he said. "They told me you weren't feeling quite the ticket and had stayed in bed, but I must say, you look marvelous. One of Céleste's?"

"Yes. This is the first time I've had it on, but I felt like celebrating being at home with you, again, uncle! How comfortable it is! If only we could get rid of my aunt and cousins!"

"What's that?" he had extracted a fine bowl, and was turning it this way and that. "What's that about your aunt?"

"If only we could encourage her and her offspring to go home! We are so cozy by ourselves, are we not?"

"Nothing simpler! Tell them we're going to Brimford for a spot of hunting and taking Cook. She won't stay here if she knows she won't be getting her creams every day!"

Brimford was her uncle's hunting lodge in Leicestershire, conveniently situated for the Quorn hunt.

"Oh, I say, do you think we could? What have you heard about it this year? Is the scent running high?"

"No, It's been a damned poor show, apparently, but she doesn't know that! The only thing will be to keep that young Chauncey from asking to come. At best he'd put us to the blush, and at worst, he'd break his neck."

"I think he may be so pleased with his new phaeton he'll be glad to go home and show it off."

"That's settled then. I'll bring it up tonight at dinner. You're right. It will be nice to have the place back to ourselves, I must say." Uncle Leonard replaced the bowl and took out a vase.

"You're happy here with me, aren't you, uncle? You don't wish for other , er… female companionship?"

"Whatever can you mean?" her uncle looked shocked at what he thought she might be suggesting.

"Oh no, I don't mean anything like that!" Trixie gave a little laugh. "It's just, I wondered if you were thinking of getting married?"

"Me? Getting married? Why on earth should you think that?" Now she had his whole attention.

"It's that I thought you were becoming particularly attentive to the Baroness."

"The Baroness? Was I? I hope I've been polite, nothing more. You don't think I've been giving her ideas, do you?" He looked aghast at the idea.

"No, I can assure you, you haven't. In fact I got a note from Margarethe today saying her mother is engaged to Arthur Witherspoon."

Leonard looked relieved. "Can't say I'm surprised. He had a *tendre* for her years ago."

"So you're not disappointed?"

"Disappointed? Of course not! Why should I be? I wish them every joy. They'll do well together. He's a good fellow, but an old fogey, and she's frightfully proper, you know. I like a woman with a little more spirit! Like you, my dear." He kissed her affectionately on the cheek.

After the shock of the letter she had received, Trixie felt her eyes fill with tears. She blinked them back and said, "Well, they blame me for the elopement débacle. Margarethe says we can no longer be as close as we were. Her brother made her write it, I expect. He's very proper, too."

"Don't let it upset you, Trixie," said her uncle kindly. "Those foreigners don't understand our London ways. We don't need 'em. We did very well before they arrived and will do very well without them again. What does the brother look like, anyway? I haven't met him, have I?"

"No, you haven't. He only just got here. He's very tall and good-looking. Blond, like his sister. You'd easily recognize him."

"Good, I shall avoid him in the clubs. That's the thing to do. Avoid the lot of them! Don't let them bother us!"

Trixie gave her uncle an impetuous hug. "Oh, uncle! You are a dear!"

Foljambe came into the library at that point and gave a slight cough.

"Mr. Cornelius Wolfson is in the small parlor, my lady. He did not wish to be put in the drawing room with your cousins."

In fact, Corny had slipped the butler a *douceur* and asked him not to broadcast his arrival. He had something private to say to Lady Trixie. Foljambe did not approve of Cornelius any more than he had approved of the other young men who had come to have private conversations with her ladyship. But he did approve of the *douceurs* he received.

"Thank you, Foljambe. I'm coming now."

On her way to the parlor, Trixie wondered how she could have been so wrong about her uncle and the Baroness. Still, at least breaking the news about her engagement hadn't been a problem. She hoped Corny wouldn't be annoyed at the warning she was about to give him.

"Trixie!" said her friend, who was looking uneasy when she came into the parlor. He gave her a bow that was a little more ragged than his usual graceful performance. "I'm glad you're home. You missed Lady March's the other night and I wondered… er… thing is, Trixie…."

She was looking at him in some surprise. Since when did Corny bow to her?

He began again, on a different note. "I say, you look as fine as fivepence! That's a mighty pretty gown!"

He broke off again, and ran his finger around his neck cloth, as if it were choking him. "Er… glad you sent me that note. I, er… I want to talk to you."

"I want to talk to you, too," she said. "Whatever's the matter with you, Corny? Sit down, for heaven's sake!"

"Yes, But… er, if you don't mind, Trixie, I'd rather stay standing. Thing is, something I want to say and prefer to get it off m' chest."

"Well, say it then. Stop humming and hawing. Get on with it."

To her intense surprise and embarrassment, Cornelius dropped down on one knee and grabbed her hand.

"Here it is then: Trixie, will you marry me? I've wanted to ask you for some time, but couldn't get to the sticking point. Then, when you sent that note, told m'self perhaps you'd guessed and were trying to help me out. You're always helping people, and I thought, well, why not me?"

Trixie was aghast. "Marry you? What on earth are you talking about? Get up! You look ridiculous!"

"Well, I must say, Trixie!" Cornelius leaped to his feet. "You don't give a feller much credit. Damned hard thing to do, y'know, proposin'. Bound to look like a fool."

Trixie saw the truth in what he was saying and was sorry for her response. "I'm sorry, Corny," she said, "but you took me by complete surprise. I was going to tell you I've found out Margarethe's brother is a real stick in the mud and if you were going to propose to her, you'd better be ready for some pretty stiff questioning. But I see now I was quite beside the point."

"I should say so! Marry Margarethe? Whatever put that idea in your head? Pretty girl and all that. Make someone a lovely wife, but not me! Too strait-laced for my taste! Anyway, I've been in love with you for years! You have to know that!"

"Oh, Corny! How can you say that when not so very long ago you were dropping worms down my back!"

"Just like you to remember that at a moment like this," retorted Cornelius bitterly. "You don't still resent me for that, do you?"

"Of course not! But I haven't thought of you as a husband, either! Does your Mama know you've proposed to me? She doesn't like me very much, you know."

"I'll deal with Mama, thank you. Now, Trixie, will you or won't you?"

"Oh, no, Corny, I won't. I can't," she cried.

Then she realized what she was doing. Cornelius had proposed to her in the time-honored fashion. She should reply in the same way.

"I mean, thank you, Cornelius. I am truly sensible of the honor you do me in asking me to become your wife, but I'm afraid I must decline. We should not suit."

"Stuff!" snorted Cornelius. "Of course we should suit. We've been friends for ever. You don't love me, that's it, isn't it?"

She had to be honest. "I'm afraid it is, Corny. You are a good and dear friend, but I don't love you. Not in that way."

"That's it then," said Cornelius, suddenly very dignified. "In that case, I wish you goodnight, Lady Beatrix. No need to see me out. I know the way."

He bowed, went to the door and opened it, nearly causing the butler, who had his ear pressed to it, to fall into the room.

"If you're expecting another tip, Foljambe," said Cornelius with some hauteur, "you aren't going about it the right way." And he stalked straight past him.

Trixie sank onto a chair, her head in her hands. Cornelius wanted to marry her, and her uncle had no *tendre* for the Baroness! How could she have been so wrong?

Chapter Twenty-Eight

A few days later the Countess, Chauncey, Mariah and of course, Pug, went home, all well satisfied with their London sojourn. The Countess was pleased with her gowns and impatient to show them off to her less fortunate neighbors in the country. As Trixie had surmised, Chauncey was looking forward to demonstrating his prowess with his phaeton and pair, and Leonard had insisted he take the showy saddle horse as well. Truth be told, he wanted the slug out of his stables.

His nephew couldn't believe his luck. He had previously been forced to ride the indifferent hacks provided by his father, who knew as well as Leonard what a poor whip he was. Now he felt like a warrior returning home. He had arrived in the big old fashioned coach his mother preferred, and here he was, driving his own equipage, with a groom astride the good-looking mount that was also his. Like his mother, he couldn't wait to show off.

Mariah was looking forward to telling her bosom-bows about what she had learned from Trixie, and sharing the books she had devoured, which her cousin had kindly bestowed upon her to keep.

Pug sat smugly on his mistress's knee, plumper than ever with the many creams he had shared. He would have been less satisfied had he realized those particular treats were now at an end.

Uncle and niece re-mounted the steps to the London house with a sigh. Thank heavens they were gone! They sat down to a pleasant luncheon *à deux* and discussed what to do with the rest of the day. Leonard was going to the sales rooms where he hoped to purchase another piece for his collection.

"Old Montforte is sniffing around it," he said. "But I'm going to offer a hefty pre-sale price. Won't he be surprised when I steal a march on him!"

The Earl of Montforte was Leonard's chief competitor in the *sang de boeuf* market and nothing pleased either more than outdoing the other.

Trixie was still suffering from the failure of her matchmaking plans, and she had not yet recovered from being cast off by the von Schwerins. She and her uncle were invited to a rout party that evening and she supposed they would be there. For a moment, she considered crying off, but then decided it would be up to them to stay away if they did to wish to see her. It was they, after all, who had declared the rupture.

"I think I'll go to Céleste's," she said, resolutely pushing these disturbing ideas from her mind, "and see if Juliette can make me a new riding bonnet."

Juliette had a positive genius for creating exactly the thing. She was horribly expensive, but Trixie didn't give that a thought.

The bonnet she had worn on the abortive trip to Hatfield was drooping sadly. Six hours in an open carriage had not treated it kindly. But she didn't mention her reasons for needing a new one. She didn't want to mention Lukas von Schwerin.

Later in the afternoon, having given her groom orders to walk the horses, Trixie climbed gracefully down from her carriage and entered the establishment of *C et J, Modes Parisiennes*. A group of ladies was on one side of the elegant salon, discussing something in hushed voices. When she came in, the conversation ceased immediately and all eyes were turned on her. She thought it a little odd, but merely nodded to them all in a friendly way before crossing the room to where Céleste had emerged, having heard the tinkle of the bell over the door.

"Milady!" said Céleste, "'ow may I 'elp you today? You require a new gown, perhaps, for your *fiançailles?*"

"*Fiançailles?* Whatever are you talking about?" Trixie had a sudden thought that Corny had talked openly of an engagement between them. But no, he would never have done that!

"Oh, eet eez nozzing! I am mistook, pardonnez-moi."

"You certainly are! I have no engagement on the horizon, I can assure you! No, I have come for a new bonnet. Is Juliette available?"

"But of course, I take you to her."

Céleste led Trixie into a mirrored ante-chamber where a number of lovely bonnets were displayed on stands. A matron whom she knew well was trying on a wide-brimmed confection, much too young for her, and Juliette was wrinkling her nose, a sure sign to anyone who knew her that she disapproved the selection.

The matron saw Trixie enter and there was a distinct straightening of her back, a sure sign to anyone who knew *her* that she was seeing something or someone of whom *she* disapproved.

"Thank you," she said, removing the bonnet from her steel grey curls, "That will be all for today."

And looking Trixie up and down haughtily, she sailed out of the room.

Puzzled, Trixie watched her go, then she turned with a little laugh. "Whatever can I have done this time?" she said more to herself than Juliette. "Truly, one only has to march a little out of step to incur the displeasure of those gorgons who line the walls of every ball for the sole purpose of disapproving!"

Juliette gave the enigmatic shrug for which the French are so famous. She had heard rumors about Lady Beatrix, but she wasn't about to voice them. She was much too good a customer.

They spent the next half hour discussing the relative merits of this style and that, eventually deciding on a neat riding bonnet with a small curly brim like the old one, except that the brim at the back was turned right up against the back of the head. From it an amber feather could be set so that it curled forward over the crown. Juliette declared this a new and more sophisticated look, and Trixie could only agree. The milliner would make it up for her and send it over in a day or two.

A lad was sent to find her ladyship's carriage, and a few minutes later she left, again nodding at the huddled group that once more fell silent as she passed.

Chapter Twenty-Nine

Since she had so far not worn it out of the house, for that evening's rout party Trixie arrayed herself in her amber evening gown again. Everyone who had seen it had told her how well it became her. She had her maid arrange her hair on the top of her head with a rather elaborate diamond-edged comb that had belonged to her mother. There was to be no dancing, so this was not inappropriate, though it was, perhaps, a little more than the occasion warranted. She wanted to look particularly fine. If the von Schwerins had decided to cast her off, let them see she neither desired nor needed them!

She was conscious as she entered the room on the arm of her uncle that a hush fell on the company and people looked their way, but knowing she looked her best, she put it down to her appearance. Uncle Leonard noticed nothing because he was immediately drawn into conversation with the competitor for the *sang de boeuf* piece, who demanded to know if he had any idea why it had been withdrawn from the sale at the last moment.

Trixie walked forward alone and was surprised but not displeased when Cornelius Wolfson came straight across the room and urgently took her arm.

"Come over here," he said, pulling her towards a sofa in the corner of the room behind a potted palm.

"You're not going to renew your addresses, are you, Corny?" she said with a laugh.

"Certainly not, and you might have told me about it before I proposed like an idiot!"

Trixie was astonished. "Told you about what?"

"About how you compromised yourself with that von Schwerin feller. At least, everyone is saying it was him you were seen with leaving the inn." Cornelius was bitter.

"I compromised myself wi...?"

But even as she said it, Trixie suddenly understood. The women in the milliner's, the matron cutting her, the hush that fell over the room just now, all of it. Someone had seen her and Lukas in Hatfield and that someone had broadcast the news.

She sank down onto the sofa. "You have to believe me, Corny," she said earnestly looking up at him, "I didn't tell you because I hadn't done anything of the sort. I didn't compromise myself. It's true I went to Hatfield with Lukas von Schwerin, but we were pursuing his sister and Chauncey. We thought they were eloping."

"You mean Margarethe, the same sister you tried to fob off on me?" Cornelius was irate. "I must say, Trixie, I thought better of you! If you prefer some blond god to me, at least, that's what they're saying he is, all well and good, but to push his sister on me after she's run off with Chauncey, that's beyond enough. I've known you forever, Trixie, and you've always had an odd kick in your gallop, but this... well!" Words failed him.

"But I didn't, Corny! I didn't! Well, I did think Margarethe might be a good match for you, though now I see I was wrong. But she didn't elope with Chauncey, that's the whole point! We *thought* she had and went after her, then had an accident and had to stay at an inn till the wheel of the curricle was repaired. It was all perfectly innocent!"

"Innocent, is it, to appear in public in broad daylight with your hair all anyhow, in clothing that looked like it had been slept in? To tell the innkeeper he's your half-brother, when we all know you have no such thing? To have him pay your shot?"

Trixie was nearly in tears. "We made up the story about him being a half-brother to allay suspicions! I forgot about paying, and anyway, all I had was a few shillings in my reticule. I couldn't pay! Ask him yourself!"

"That's just it, he ain't here. None of them are here. Looks like they're too ashamed to show their faces. I'm amazed to see you here, to tell the truth."

"Not here? But…."

Just then, Uncle Leonard appeared, looking unusually grave. "Oh, here you are, Trixie. Cornelius." He gave the young man a slight bow. "Come to take you home, my dear. Shouldn't have insisted you come, knowing you had the headache. I've had the carriage brought round."

He urged Trixie to her feet, and put her arm over his, patting it with old-world courtesy. She rose without a word and in spite of every instinct, walked slowly, her head held high, across the room. They appeared in no hurry. Leonard bowed and smiled to acquaintances as they passed, and Trixie did her best to follow suit.

The last thing they heard as they left the salon was a raised female voice saying sardonically, "She wasn't wearing that diamond comb at the inn, I'll be bound. From what I hear, she looked as if she had just scrambled out of her nightgown!"

A hoot of derisive laughter echoed in Trixie's ears as she forced herself not to run to the carriage.

Chapter Thirty

It was as much as Trixie could do not to completely break down on the ride home.

"Everyone believes the worst of me, uncle! What can we do?" she cried. "It's all so unfair! We didn't do anything! The Baron doesn't even *like* me!"

"Everyone likes you, Trixie!" was all Leonard could think to say.

"That's not true! You heard them! Some of those women are positively delighting in seeing me shamed!" Tears began to roll down her face. "You heard what that one said as we were leaving! My hair was in a mess! Of course it was! I had no maid and I can't manage it myself! I hate it!" She tore at her elegant coiffure and ripped the comb out of her hair. "Thank goodness my mother isn't alive to see this!" She turned the diamond-studded ornament over and over in her hands, tears falling freely now.

Her uncle patted her shoulder and murmured soothing sounds. He had avoided close relationships with women all his life and had no experience of weeping females. Trixie had hardly ever cried, even as a child, and since growing up, never did so. It broke his soft heart to see her, but he had no idea how to comfort her.

But when they arrived home, he thoughtfully pulled the hood of Trixie's evening cloak over her head and led her indoors, saying to Foljambe, "Lady Beatrix has the headache. Call her maid to meet her upstairs. Or rather, call Miss Wood. She'll know what to do."

When Hester Wood came into Trixie's room a few minutes later, she found her sobbing into her pillow. She sat quietly patting her back until the paroxysm passed. Then she listened without comment to the younger woman's tale, interrupted as it was by shuddering sobs. Hetty knew about the wild goose chase with the Baron, and believed her absolutely when she said nothing improper had occurred. She now heard about the snubbing in the hat shop, the conversations falling silent when she appeared, Corny's revelation and, almost worst of all, the ribald remark spoken loud enough for everyone to hear as she was leaving the party.

"Oh, Hetty!" she cried, "I don't know what to do or say! I can deny it all I want, but people will believe what they want to believe. I wish I knew if the Baron has heard the rumors, and if he has denied them. None of the von Schwerins were there this evening. Of course, for a man it's different. The gentlemen will just think he's a bold fellow, and the women will probably admire him for being a rake. You know how it is! The mamas will warn the girls off, and that will make him all the more attractive! It's *so unfair*!"

"Yes, it is, my dear," agreed her old governess. "We women bear the brunt of all misfortune much more than the gentlemen. But you have described the Baron as being very upright and proper. Therefore people will believe him when he denies the accusations. You see, it will be a nine-days wonder."

"Perhaps I should leave town immediately. Uncle and I can go to Brimford, after all. Yes, that's what we'll do. I'll see him in the morning. I don't think I can bear to talk any more about it tonight."

Privately, Hetty thought that if Beatrix left town, it would serve to confirm rather than deny the rumors, but she said nothing. She helped Trixie get ready for bed, brought her some hot milk with a drop of laudanum, and sat by her until she fell asleep.

Trixie slept late the next morning and took her tea and bread and butter in bed. She knew Uncle Leonard was not an early riser, and was particular about his toilette, so did not think of seeing him much before noon. Accordingly, it was gone eleven when she made her way downstairs, and she had just settled in the small family parlor, having sent Foljambe to see when her uncle could receive her, when the front door knocker sounded.

She knew one of the footmen would answer the door and was not surprised to hear a brief conversation. The other voice sounded familiar, but no one came to find her, so obviously it was not a visitor for her. Thank goodness. She didn't think she could face anyone. She knew she was looking far from her best. She had shadows under her eyes and was so pale she had been forced to pinch her cheeks to have any color at all.

The house fell silent. Trixie sat there for perhaps a quarter of an hour, trying not to think of the events of the day before, but unable to think of anything else. Then she heard the sound of steps on the stairs. To her astonishment and intense dismay, when the parlor door opened, Lukas von Schwerin stepped in with her uncle right behind him.

The butler hovered in the doorway until Leonard said, in a dismissive voice quite unlike his normal tone, "Thank you, Foljambe, that will be all. You may close the door and return to your post."

Her uncle knew of the butler's predilection for listening at doors, and clearly did not want this to be one of those occasions.

Lukas von Schwerin clicked his heels and bowed, saying "Lady Beatrix, good morning."

She was still too astonished and dismayed to do anything other than return a mechanical curtsey and a muttered response. Even the heel clicking failed to penetrate her befogged brain.

"Trixie, my dear, sit down," said her uncle, sitting down on the sofa himself and patting the seat next to him. Then he waved vaguely at the chairs. "Von Schwerin, my boy, sit, sit!"

My boy? The term astounded Trixie, and she turned to look at her uncle, who smiled broadly at her. "Trixie," he said, "I'm delighted to tell you, you have received a most advantageous offer from the Baron von Schwerin. He has explained his very considerable…." Leonard halted, not wanting to use the word *fortune,* "er, possessions, and has said everything right and proper in professing his urgent desire to marry you."

"*Marry* me?" exclaimed Trixie. "But he doesn't even *like* me!"

She turned to Lukas, "You don't *want* to marry me! You think you are honor bound to marry me, that's it, isn't it?"

"Trixie!" her uncle frowned. "The Baron has expressed himself most correctly. He recognizes the unfortunate position he has put you in and wishes to do what any gentleman would do to put it right."

"Uncle! I beg you to let him speak for himself!" she turned to Lukas again. "On the way to Hatfield you said a woman's honor is fragile. You think I cannot weather the storm of being thought to have spent the night with you. So you offer me marriage, even though you find me foolish. Why, a week ago you were forbidding your sister to have anything to do with me!"

He made a movement as if to speak, but Trixie continued hotly, "Do not deny it. I perceived your voice at the back of her letter."

"I assure you, Lady Beatrix," he said, when she stopped long enough to allow him to speak, "that letter was entirely of her own devising. Our mother defended you, but Margarethe wished to draw back from the closeness you and she had enjoyed. In fact, I was of the opinion that knowing you as she now does, there could be no danger of her following your unconventional precepts too closely."

"Oh, thank you!" cried Trixie. "She could continue to see me because I could no longer do her any harm! Is that what you mean?"

"I did not put it as baldly as that, but yes, I suppose that's what I meant."

"And this is the sort of woman you wish to marry? A foolish one who is likely to be a danger to her uninitiated sisters?"

"No," replied he Baron gently. "The woman I wish to marry is one I know puts the welfare of others ahead of herself. Why else would she run after her cousin in so hot-headed a fashion? She is often foolish and intemperate, but she is kind. I think marriages have been based on far less. I agree I am not romantic, I do not profess my undying love, but believe it or not, Lady Beatrix, I do like you and sometimes I even admire you. I think we will deal well enough together. I don't look for more."

These words struck ice into Trixie's heart. She knew she had been in love with Lukas von Schwerin from the moment she met him. Until this last dreadful day, he had occupied her thoughts almost constantly. And now, here he was, offering her not love, but a pale liking and admiration.

"Well, I do!" she said, standing up. "If it's true I'm foolish and intemperate, then know this: the man I marry will love me for it. He will love me for my faults as well as my qualities. So no, Baron, I will not marry you. I will not even say, as convention demands, that I am sensible of the honor you do me, for you do me no honor to offer me your name when your feelings towards me are so insultingly insipid."

Both men had risen when she did. Now her uncle took her hand. "But my dear," he said, "think a little. You may never again receive such a distinguishing offer. Once the rumors and gossips have done their worst, you will find few men willing to take you on."

"Then I shall die an old maid."

"If that is your final answer, I shall wish you good day," said Lukas. "But please know that I made the offer in good faith. I was as much to blame as you for engaging in that foolish escapade, and I should be sorry to see you ruined because of it. But neither will I offer you false coin. Like you, I declare you must take me as I am. I am a soldier, not a poet. Honor is more important to me than love."

He clicked his heels, bowed, and turned to leave.

"Oh, for heaven's sake, stop clicking your heels like that!" cried Trixie. "It really is ridiculous! This is London, not Prussia!"

"As I said, Lady Beatrix," answered the Baron turning back with a slight smile, "You must take me as I am."

And he went to the door, quietly opened it, and left.

Chapter Thirty-One

"I cannot help but say I think you're making a mistake, my dear," said her uncle. They had both sunk down onto the sofa. "He is a most good-looking and, yes, I must say it, wealthy young man. He owns two large estates, one in Mecklenburg-Schwerin and one here. One could never accuse him of being a fortune hunter. I daresay he is a little stiff, but in your company he would unbend in time."

"There isn't enough time in the world for him to unbend, uncle! Anyway, you heard him, he doesn't love me."

"Oh, love!" Leonard flapped his hands. "Love has so many faces!"

"Haven't you missed having someone who loves you above all? Who knows you for what you are and loves you anyway?"

"Why, I've had you, my dear!" said her uncle. "You love me, don't you? In spite of my ways?"

"Of course I do!" Trixie kissed his cheek. "We shall be as happy as grigs together! What do we need of wealthy Barons, or anyone else? Oh, uncle, let's go to Brimford after all! We need a good gallop to chase away these unhappy thoughts. Hetty says this will be a nine-days wonder, so let's go for nine days, and when we come back, all will be well!"

Her uncle received this suggestion willingly and the next couple of days were spent in preparation for a prolonged stay in the country.

But just as they were thinking they would leave on the morrow, they had an unwelcome visitor in the person of the Earl of Shelby.

The Earl was of a dyspeptic disposition and as lean as his wife was rotund. It was probably her insistence on a rich diet that upset his digestion, and he often said he never felt better than when she was away. Then he could eat a slice of bread and cheese with a little broth for lunch and dinner, and feel better than he had in months.

He hated to leave his home, for he was convinced no one could manage the estate better than he. This was probably true, for the yields were greater now than they had ever been under his late father, and certainly under his defunct brother, who preferred cards to crops and gambling to green fields. He was generally an agreeable gentleman so long as things went his way, but he had a great sense of propriety and family honor.

It has already been remarked that Mariah had not been permitted to read novels while at home. Like the Baron, her father thought them a pernicious influence on the minds of young women. He had not at first been aware that his daughter had returned home with Trixie's gift of this forbidden material. The first he had heard about it came from the local squire who called on him one day to complain that his daughter, a year younger than Mariah, had been caught reading some damn-fool nonsense given to her by her friend. She had been mooning about the house talking about *falling in love* and being carried off by a poet across the moors on a white horse. He wanted to know what the Earl meant by it, allowing his daughter to corrupt the younger generation of the neighborhood.

The Earl's wrath had been swift and terrible. Mariah had been made to surrender the books; she had been confined to the house and forbidden all outings for the foreseeable future. Her outcry had been even more terrible. She had wailed and drummed her heels, fallen into a faint, and finally been carried to her bed by two footmen.

"I want cousin Trixie!" she wailed. "No one else understands me! She's allowed to read novels! Why can't I?"

Her mother was utterly unable to deal with her, in fact, she too, had taken to her bed prostrated with her nerves. As we know, this was actually not an uncommon situation, but on this occasion, Mariah was held to blame, and through Mariah, Trixie.

The Earl was consequently in an extremely ill humor when he arrived in London. Luckily for him, Uncle Leonard was from home when his infuriated brother arrived. He immediately called for his niece and subjected her to the full force of his ire.

"How dare you, niece, expose my daughter to reading material you knew was expressly forbidden?" he cried.

"But uncle, I didn't know it was forbidden. Mariah never mentioned it. No more did my aunt. She read them too! And honestly, I don't think there's anything wrong with the novels! Uncle Leonard never had an objection to them!"

"Then Leonard is much to blame. I know he's always been a fool as far as you are concerned, and see where it has led us! For me to have the Squire accuse me of allowing my daughter to mislead his! Me! I tell you, Beatrix! I never thought to see the day!"

"I'm truly sorry, uncle!" said Trixie, not knowing what to offer in mitigation. "Should I write to the Squire and tell him it's all my fault?"

"Certainly not! You have done enough, quite enough! It only remains for me to decide whether you should continue under this roof, where, it seems, you are subject to no control at all!"

Having delivered himself of this bombshell, much to the relief of the whole household, the Earl took himself off to his club. When Leonard came home, he was inclined to take a light view of the threat.

"For we both know, my dear," he said, "He cannot have you at Shelby Court. The Countess has repeatedly said she would not be able to live with you."

"But Uncle, he was truly furious. If he absolutely puts his foot down, she will have to accept what he says!"

"Tosh, tosh," said Uncle Leonard. "Be easy, nothing will come of it, you'll see."

But he was wrong. Worse was to come.

Chapter Thirty-Two

Leonard and Trixie were sitting quietly by the fire, she rather inexpertly knotting a fringe, and he examining the new auction catalog, when the Earl erupted into the drawing room, Foljambe running behind him.

"Niece!" he thundered, for once so angry he didn't stop to consider that the butler could hear every word, "What is this I now hear about you spending the night at an inn in Hatfield with some man or other? Is there no end to your perfidy? Are you determined to ruin us all?"

"But, but, uncle, I didn't!"

"Thank you, Foljambe. You may return to your post." Uncle Leonard spoke with unusual sternness.

"What? Yes, remove yourself, man." Then the Earl returned to Trixie. "Well, that's what they're all saying at the club, and by God, there's no smoke without fire!"

"It's true I spent the night in Hatfield, and it's true the Baron von Schwerin was with me, but we were not together, at least, we were, but not like that!"

"What do you mean? You were together but you weren't?"

Trixie was forced to tell him the whole story.

"You mean you thought Chauncey, my son Chauncey, had eloped with this young woman? What more shame are you determined to bring on our name?"

"It was all a mistake! He did not elope, the Baron and I did not spend the night together. It's just a malicious rumor!"

"Well, there's some comfort that Chauncey was not involved, but as far as you are concerned, my girl, rumor or not, the damage is done. Who is this Baron? He must be made to marry you. Either that, or you will come to Shelby Court and spend the rest of your life there. If you're lucky, a local man may take a shine to you, if he's not too particular. By God, Trixie, you've done it this time!"

"The Baron did offer for her," said Uncle Leonard into the silence that followed this declaration. "But Trixie wouldn't have him."

"Wouldn't have him? Wouldn't have him? What choice does she have? Where is he? Let him be brought here. Let's see if we can persuade him to repeat his offer. I hope you weren't too absolute in your refusal of him!"

"I was!" Tears were by now running down Trixie's cheeks. "I said I wouldn't marry him because he didn't love me! And I still won't! You can't make me!"

"Love? Stuff! That's where you are wrong, my lady! You may not be aware of it, but your fortune is held in trust until you marry and I am the Trustee. I have been generous up till now, too generous it appears. I shall not be in the future. You have two options: marriage with this Baron, if he'll still have you, or spending your days in the country where, believe me, you will have no access to the sort of life you have been wont to lead here in London. I will have no shamed niece of mine disporting herself in public, believe me!"

Trixie broke down entirely, and sobbed. Soft hearted Uncle Leonard attempted to console her, but his older brother, made of much sterner stuff, went into the hall to find out from Foljambe where this Baron might be found. But the butler had gone downstairs to deliver the news to the housekeeper that Lady Beatrix had done it this time, and her uncle was pitching it hot. The Earl returned to the drawing room and furiously rang the bell.

"Typical of your household, Leonard! No butler in the hall! God dammit, you live like gypsies, the pair of you! The sooner Beatrix is out of here and learning some propriety, the better!"

"That is unfair, uncle!" cried Trixie, her tears suspended in hot defense of her beloved uncle. "Anyway, I can give you the Baron's direction. You don't need to involve Foljambe. I'm surprised you should think that proper!"

She ran to the standish, scratched the Baron's address on a piece of paper and thrust it at him.

The Earl went to the library and wrote a brief note to Lukas von Schwerin requesting him to visit them at his earliest convenience the next day. Then he went to bed.

Uncle Leonard sat with Trixie in the drawing room trying to find a solution to the dreadful choice that faced Trixie, for they both knew that as head of the family, the Earl's decision would be final. Then they too went upstairs to bed. It was impossible for either of them to find sleep until the early hours when, exhausted, they fell into a slumber, from which neither awoke refreshed.

Her maid brought Trixie a note from the Earl that he was expecting the Baron von Schwerin at eleven that morning. She was to be ready to receive him.

Chapter Thirty-Three

When Lukas pulled the bell at the Shelby townhouse, he was immediately shown into the library where the Earl was awaiting him. Mutual introductions were made, since the men did not know each other, but there was no exchange of pleasantries. Neither man had a desire for friendship. The Earl strode back and forth across the room, evidently in the grip of powerful emotions, and then addressed the visitor.

"You will forgive my plain speaking, Baron, but I understand that you and my niece Beatrix spent the night in Hatfield together earlier this week. We need not discuss the nature of the circumstances; the effect on our family honor is the same. I'm sure you understand that."

Lukas nodded.

"I also understand that as a consequence you made her an offer of marriage. This was refused."

"Yes," said Lukas, shortly.

"And are you prepared to make that offer again?"

He raised his eyebrows at the question, but after a hesitation replied, "I am."

"I'm exceedingly obliged to you," bowed the Earl. "You understand the situation I am in."

"I do."

The Earl went to the bell, and when Foljambe came in, instructed him to fetch Lady Beatrix.

The two men sat in silence until Trixie arrived. She was not looking her best. She was pale, with dark shadows under her eyes, but she held her head high and walked with a firm step.

"Further to what we discussed last night, Beatrix," said the Earl, "the Baron has generously agreed to renew his offer of marriage. Are you now willing to accept it?"

"It appears I have no choice."

Lukas narrowed his eyes. "Am I to understand you are being coerced into accepting my proposal, Lady Beatrix?"

"More or less, yes. My uncle has made it clear that I may either become your wife or live in permanent seclusion in the country. It seems he controls my fortune and can make my existence very restricted."

"And of the two evils, becoming my wife seems the lesser, is that it?" There was a humor in Lukas's tone that surprised her.

When Trixie made no answer, he turned to her uncle.

"My lord, may I ask you to leave us?" he said, "I think my prospective fiancée and I need a few moments alone. I presume her honor can be no more tarnished than it already is."

The Earl bowed in agreement and left the room.

"Sit down, Trixie," said Lukas, surprising her again, this time with the use of her nickname. "Let us be honest with each other."

He led her to a small sofa that stood on one side of the room.

"You were incensed the other day when I said I didn't love you, and yet I was prepared to marry you. If you can put to one side for a moment the newly fashionable idea that love is a pre-requisite for marriage, you will see that what I offer is no different from what generations of men have offered generations of women. I would give you the protection of my name and a security you will scarcely have without marriage. And I don't dislike you; I've already said I find much in you to admire. But I don't know you. How can I love you?"

Because, God help me, I'm not even sure I like you, but I love you. I can't help it! was what immediately flashed into her mind, but tears starting to her eyes, what she said was, "It's not how I imagined my future husband would address me, talking of security, protection, and admiration. What need have I of any of those?"

"You mean they don't sound *romantic* enough for you? You see, you are more influenced by those novels than you think."

For the first time in their acquaintance, Lukas gave her his charming smile.

"Perhaps you have no need of them now," he said in a gentle voice, "but can't you imagine a time when you might? I know you've lived all your life in peace and the safety of a loving household. But I've seen dreadful times when families were torn apart by war. Then security and protection are as important as love, in fact, even indistinguishable from it."

He took her hand. "For the sake of both your honor and mine, marry me, Trixie," he said softly. "I promise to do my best to be a good husband. I won't interfere with you or your fortune. But you must try to be more conventional, not set the town by its ears, and remember you have a husband whose life experience has made him very different from you."

He smiled at her again, and understanding for the first time how his experience had shaped his view of the world, she smiled too.

"Yes, Lukas," she said slowly. "For your honor and mine I will marry you, and I will try not to disgrace you, though I don't suppose I shall always succeed."

"No, I imagine not," he chuckled. But then, standing up before her, he bowed and said, "But I believe the conventional reply is that you make me the happiest of men."

He raised her hand to his lips and kissed her fingertips. But he did not attempt to kiss her.

Chapter Thirty-Four

The notice of the engagement of the Lady Beatrix Shelby and the Baron Lukas von Schwerin appeared in the papers the following day. Notes of congratulation poured into the Shelby townhouse, for by now the Baron's circumstances were well known. The most fulsome compliments came, of course, from the very persons who had been loudest in criticism. The pair of women who had seen them at The Eight Bells even went so far as to tell each other that they had been the agents of the engagement, which, in truth, they had.

The couple was immediately invited to innumerable dinners and "intimate" get-togethers, which were thinly veiled attempts to obtain details of how the couple met. The Baron had been unknown in town and how Trixie had met him and conquered his heart was a matter for considerable conjecture. The story of the night at the inn was embroidered out of all recognition until it resembled the plot of one of the romance novels the prospective groom so disliked.

Trixie and Lukas turned smiling faces to all the enquiries, direct and oblique, saying only they had met through Margarethe, who was well known to be Trixie's friend.

The next subject of conjecture was when they would marry. Lukas did not press her for an early date and this caused Trixie both despair and relief. He obviously didn't care to be married soon and she told herself she didn't want to be wife to someone who wasn't eager for her. On the other hand, she missed him when she didn't see him and had a dreadful mixture of anxiety and longing for the day they would be wed.

She had a hard time keeping up a smiling countenance and her detractors were pleased to note she was not looking her usual blooming self. She was much more withdrawn, and Corny, who had recovered from his fit of pique and even considered himself well out of it, asked her if she was feeing quite the thing.

"Anyone would think you ain't looking forward to your wedding," he said sympathetically. "Mind you, I'd feel the same myself if I was marryin' the Baron. Bit stiff, ain't he? I say," he added with an unusual burst of perspicacity, "they ain't forcing you to marry him, are they?"

She wouldn't admit even to Corny that he had put his finger on the problem.

"Of course not," she replied lightly. "There was nothing in all that, as I told you. No, it has all been a bit of a whirlwind and I don't think my feet have quite touched ground yet."

An unfortunate increase in attention to the von Schwerin family was provided by the announcement that the Baroness and the Honorable Arthur Witherspoon were married. They had exchanged vows in a private family ceremony in the local parish church. Not many people knew of their involvement, and coming on the heels of the announcement about Lukas and Beatrix, it caused a good deal of ribald comment in the salons and clubs.

"'Pon my soul," a gentleman was heard to say in one of the clubs, "those von Schwerins wasted no time. Cut a swathe through London! Just like Napoleon through Europe! I suppose the gel will be next. Who's she got her eye on?" Then, his gaze alighting on the scion of an old family who happened to be lounging there, "Not you, is it, young Fotheringay?"

"Sorry, sir, what?" replied the young man. He was just going up to Oxford for the Michaelmas term and had no idea what the gentleman was talking about.

"The von Schwerin girl. You marryin' her?"

"Me, sir?" the boy was taken aback. "I've never met her!"

"That don't seem to be an obstacle if what we hear about the rest of the family is true. You watch out, Fotheringay. Find yourself leg-shackled to Margarethe von Schwerin before you can say knife!"

Word of this came to Lukas's ears and infuriated him. Was the von Schwerin name never to be off people' lips? His mother and her new husband had left for a wedding trip in Paris and would be moving into her husband's country home when they returned. He decided it was a good moment for the rest of the family to leave London and let the gossip die down. He would take Margarethe to Chorley House. The season was over, anyway, and he had a fancy for Christmas in the country.

"You should ask Trixie," said Margarethe. "It will be her home soon and she may like to plan some alterations."

Relations between the two young women had been strained. They met in public but rarely in private. Now Margarethe was regretting having written that letter and was eager to become friends again with her future sister-in-law.

Trixie was loth to leave Uncle Leonard, especially at Christmas, but he surprised her by saying he didn't mind being alone. There were a couple of sales he wanted to go to and he'd received an invitation from his old friend Lady March to stay for the holidays.

The truth was, he, too, was tired of the gossip in the clubs and was finding it harder and harder to turn a deaf ear to some of the more outrageous comments about his niece. He realized he had been lax in bringing her up, and her diminished spirits were a reproach to him.

So the last days of November saw the Lady Beatrix and her governess leaving for Wiltshire in a coach with Margarethe von Schwerin. The Baron had chosen to ride alongside instead of taking the curricle, so Juno was also in the coach lying on the floor and keeping the ladies' feet warm. She periodically stood and looked out the window to be sure the God of her existence was still with them, then rearranged herself with a sigh. She was content her two favorite people were there, even if not together. She could tolerate Margarethe and Hettie. The latter, who was determined to prove she was not afraid of her, timidly patted her on the head saying "Good dog!"

Of course I am, she thought scornfully, *though what it has to do with you I don't know.*

Chapter Thirty-Five

Wiltshire was a part of the country that Trixie had never seen before. Shelby Court, where, in any case, she went as infrequently as possible, was to the south in Hampshire, and she could only be happy they had no reason to go north. After her experience in Hatfield, she vowed never to go that way again. Margarethe had been raised in the German Duchy and knew nothing of England but London. They were both glad to get out of the capital.

Having left fashionable London by the Westminster Bridge, they crossed the Thames again at Kingston, driving past the ancient Kingston Guildhall and the golden statue of Queen Anne. Their destination for the night was Farnborough, with rooms at an inn Lukas had bespoken, glorying in the name of *Tumbledown Dick*.

"Oh dear, I hope it doesn't tumble on our heads," said Hettie, then with a bravery born of surviving unfortunate early life experiences, "but if it does, I daresay we shall manage."

"Trust you to say that!" replied Trixie fondly. "*We shall manage*. You've said that to me my whole life, and you know, we always have! Not that inns have fallen on our heads, of course. The worst thing I can remember is that time when I took it into my head to cut off one of my braids."

Margarethe was shocked. "Why did you do such a thing?"

"Mattie had some new scissors. They were really sharp and I experimented cutting all sorts of things, getting thicker and thicker all the time, till I finally thought of my braid. My hair is really thick, you know. But the scissors went through it like butter!"

"So I suppose you could say it was a scientific experiment," said Margarethe. "It was the sign of a lively mind."

"That's kind of you to say. But it looked awful! My hair was totally lopsided: short on one side and long on the other. We tried everything, but in the end we just had to cut off the other braid as well. Luckily, my hair curls, and I simply wore a cap until my hair grew."

"So, as Miss Wood said, you managed. I'm sure you always will. You're so competent, Trixie."

Then Margarethe took her hand.

"Oh, Trixie, I hope we can be friends again. I've so regretted sending you that letter. Mama and Lukas said I should not, but I was so upset…."

"So it wasn't your brother you were quoting?"

"No, quite the opposite."

"He said he had not encouraged you to write it, but I didn't believe him. He was so stern and disapproving of me on the trip to Hatfield. He said he deplored our friendship."

"Lukas never lies," said Margarethe, "even to save someone's feelings. You always know where you are with him. And yes, he does seems strict and disapproving, but it's because he has so many burdens to carry. He has our mother and me to provide for and keep safe. You've no idea what Europe was like after the defeat of Bonaparte at Waterloo. Displaced men without work formed bands and robbed people on the road. Our trip was really dangerous, you know. Then he has to manage our estates in

Germany and here. He has a great deal on his mind. And all this comes on the heels of being forced to fight in wars, first on one side, then the other, and losing our father right at the end. His experiences cause him to wake at night, you know. We hear him shouting sometimes. He always says he just had a bad dream but one time he confessed to mama that he sees our father dying and smells his blood on his hands. And then we lost our grandfather. It has been dreadful for us all, but the worst for him."

Trixie was struck again about how little she really knew of Lukas von Schwerin. She had never taken the trouble to find out any more than her uncle had told her about the family. He was right when he said how different his experience had been from hers. Perhaps he was right too, that marriage did not need to be based on love, that security was just as important. She had been safe her whole life and apart from parents she couldn't remember, had never lost anyone important to her. She had never before considered how lucky she was.

She looked unseeingly out of the window, lost in her thoughts. Margarethe and Hettie, however, were delighted to notice changes in the scenery. The land rose gently with the outcroppings of the South Downs that snake across southern England all the way to the coast. Hettie reminded Trixie of the book of maps they had studied when she was a child, with illustrations of these ancient hills. They rise in white majesty, culminating at Beachy Head in Sussex, so tall they can be seen from ships far off in the English Channel. Trixie nodded distractedly, but Margarethe listened with enthusiasm.

"Mama had told me of the white cliffs one can see at Dover and it was thrilling to see them when we crossed the Channel. I had no idea they began so far inland."

"England is full of fascinating things to see," said Hettie, ever the governess. "We are as yet still in Hampshire, but Wiltshire, where we will be going tomorrow, is well known for its evidence of ancient habitations. In fact I think if I remember correctly the word *Downs* is derived from the old English word for *Hill*. People lived here in prehistoric times. I believe the Baron said the family estate is near the village of Amesbury, in which case it is very near Stonehenge. Do you know what that is?"

When Margarethe said she did not, Hettie explained it to her appreciative audience. And so the drive passed agreeably for at least two of them, or three, if one included Juno, who was quite happy lying at their feet, listening to their chatter.

Chapter Thirty-Six

Farnborough was in darkness by the time they arrived. It appeared to be little more than a row of houses on the banks of a river of which no one, including Hettie, knew the name. At one end was the famous inn and staging post of which Lukas had already told them the name, and at the other an ancient church, subsequently discovered to be St. Peter's.

The Tumbledown Dick was apparently so called because of its association with the son of Oliver Cromwell, who tumbled from public office almost immediately after being nominated to it. It had two steeply pitched thatched roofs like an M over five upstairs bedrooms, overhanging casement windows in the front and a great air of antiquity. Inside, the ceilings were low and the flagged floors uneven. Huge wide fireplaces consumed what looked like whole trunks of trees.

Lukas had written to bespeak rooms and dinner, and just as at The Eight Bells Inn, he strode in with an air of complete command. He set the innkeeper, his wife and various bemused maids scuttling about lighting the bedroom fires, putting bricks in the beds, hot water in the jugs and tapers to the candles. No one said a word about Juno, who came and went in all the rooms, sniffing, before collapsing in front of one of the huge fireplaces.

Their stay was comfortable, and the meal surprisingly good. It featured local mutton with copious side dishes, from a dish of pike from the river (the Blackwater, as they found it was called), to a mess of leeks, cabbage cooked with apple, a pork pie, and a blackberry cream.

Lukas insisted that Hettie dine with them rather than alone. Governesses were always difficult to place; they were neither really family nor exactly staff. The Baron, however, convinced the retiring Miss Wood that she was one of the family and so enchanted her by his attention that she grew quite pink.

"My dear Trixie," she said to her later, as they were preparing for bed. "I must say I am quite delighted with the Baron. From what you had said, I expected a far more reserved gentleman. His attentions to me were kindness itself."

"Whereas to me he said nearly nothing," replied Trixie.

"But perhaps that was because you were so quiet yourself, my dear. I've never seen you like that. Do you have the headache? It's not to be wondered at, with the emotions of these last weeks. Do you get into bed and let me put some lavender water on your temples."

"Oh Hettie," Trixie burst out, voicing at last one of the thoughts that had been occupying her all day, "why is marriage considered the height of every woman's desire? I don't desire it at all! You're not married! Are you not happy?"

"I'm happy now, because I had the good fortune to be engaged by your uncle and to spend my life with you. But I do not deny that as a younger woman with no prospects of marriage, I often worried where I would go and how I would manage. The future of a single woman with neither beauty nor fortune is far from sure. Even now, knowing that soon you will no longer need me, I have some anxiety as to what will become of me."

Trixie started up from her pillow and threw her arms around the frail old lady. "How can you say such a thing, Hettie? You know I shall never let you go! You will live with me forever! Wherever I go, you will go. You need not give it another thought!"

She was horrified to see her governess remove the handkerchief she invariably kept in her sleeve and wipe her eyes.

"Don't cry, Hettie, please don't cry. Or I shall cry, too. It's all my fault! I should have thought of it before. I should have reassured you. My goodness! How unfeeling I'm discovering myself to be!"

This thought kept her awake long into the night.

The next morning the horses were put to, Juno reluctantly left the fireplace, and they continued their journey to the Chorley estate, which, as Hettie had said, was near the village of Amesbury. They stopped for a luncheon and to rest the horses at a village inn, then about two hours later they were crossing a wide plain. A stiff wind made the glass in the window frames rattle. Suddenly, Margarethe called excitedly, "Look Miss Wood! There are those stones you were telling me about yesterday!"

Sure enough, on the plains some way from the road, clearly outlined against the winter sky, were the huge stones arranged in an untidy circle, some of them joined by stones across the top, like giant doorways.

Margarethe leaned out of the window into the wind and signaled to her brother. He came to her and she said, "Oh, please, Lukas, let us visit Stonehenge! I should so love to see those stones close up."

Lukas smiled down at her. "I'm sorry, Grete, I don't like to take the horses out of our way. They are already tiring and the wind makes it worse. We should keep on. We're nearly there and it's getting late. But I promise we will come back very soon. You'll see, we'll pass all sorts of huge odd stones on the side of the road. No one knows who brought them here, or why. They aren't native to the area."

Margarethe slid the window up and sat back, disappointed.

"Never mind," said Trixie, who had heard the exchange. "He said we would come back, and you told me he's always as good as his word. I have to say, I'll be glad to get somewhere we can stay still for a few days. This is a very comfortable coach, but I feel shaken to bits. The roads have been dreadful since we left London, and the rattling of the windows is giving me a headache!"

The grey day was darkening into night as they finally left the road and drove down a lane towards a wood of dark trees. On one side they passed pens of huddled sheep under three-sided shelters, each with dark-haired dogs stationed close by. On the other, lay fields stubbled from a harvest of something unrecognizable in the gloom. Juno must have smelled they were near home, for she sat up, her ears cocked.

When they entered the wood, it took a few minutes for their eyes to become accustomed to the dark, but as the vegetation cut them off from the wind, they were immediately aware of the quiet. But what struck them most forcibly was the smell. It was a sharp, resinous odor, not unpleasant but vaguely medicinal.

Hettie sniffed appreciatively. "I declare, Trixie!" she said, "it's juniper! Doesn't it remind you of that balm we used when you had a bad cough a few winters ago?"

"Yes, it is! How odd! I don't think I've ever seen the tree before. I shall be interested to see clearly what it looks like."

Then the trees cleared abruptly and they found themselves going up a long driveway to a tall grey house whose stones seemed to gather in the last glimmer of light. Huge flambeaux burned next to the steps leading up to the main door, and as they neared, a file of servants emerged to take up their positions on the steps.

Chapter Thirty-Seven

The tall, square old house had been built a hundred and fifty years before. It was of Portland stone, weathered from its original white into the pleasant grey that glowed in the dark. Margarethe drew in her beath. Their house in Schwerin had been timbered and low; this was light and lofty.

The coach came to a halt, a footman sprang forward and opened the door, putting down the steps for the ladies to descend. There was momentary confusion inside the coach, as Margarethe pushed Trixie forward.

"You go first," she said in a low voice. You are to be the mistress of the house. Besides, you take precedence in rank."

"Don't be silly," said Trixie, but Margarethe continued to urge her forward, so she descended the steps and stopped, looking up at the house. As she hesitated, Lukas came up beside her and put his large, warm hand in the small of her back.

"Let me present the butler and housekeeper," he said. "The rest of the staff you'll get to know in time."

At the feel of his hand, Trixie felt a thrill run though her. She stood stock still until a slight pressure urged her forward.

"Beatrix, this is William Prewitt the butler and Mrs. Truly the housekeeper," he said, then to them, "I am honored to present Lady Beatrix Shelby, my fiancée."

Prewitt bowed, and Mrs. Truly curtsied. "Welcome to Chorley House, my lady," she said, taking in every element of Trixie's appearance. She had a slight flush on her face and seemed a little breathless. A most natural anxiety, thought the housekeeper. Looking at her modish pelisse and bonnet, her kid gloves and neat boots, she wondered if this city girl would be happy to make a home in the country. None of this showed on her face, however, as she greeted Margarethe and the governess, before leading them into the house.

The entrance hall was two stories high, with a carved oak staircase on either side. The last of the daylight fell onto the stone flags from a skylight high in the roof. It lit up the old oak trunk, standing where it had always stood, its copper bowl now once again filled with the last rose petals of the year. The delicate scent came to Trixie's nose as she walked past. Her senses already heightened, the perfume made her almost dizzy.

In spite of its size and imposing architecture, the house felt comfortable and lived-in. This was due as much as anything to its well-kept but slightly shabby appearance. As they were shown into the drawing room, Trixie could see that the heavy oak furniture glowed with polish, but the upholstery was faded and even worn into strings in some places. The stone floors were covered in enormous Turkish rugs, also much worn. This was a real country home with none of the elegance of London townhouses. One could collapse in riding boots on the sofas without worrying about damaging them, and an old dog could curl up on the carpet in front of the fire without being chased away. This is exactly what Juno did as soon as they arrived, plumping herself down with a sigh. She was home.

After a welcome cup of tea, Mrs. Truly took the ladies upstairs to their bedchambers. Trixie looked around with interest. The furniture was of the same massive oak design as downstairs. The tall casement windows and carved-post beds were hung with a floral design heavy linen that Mrs. Truly confided was too old to be taken down and given the good beating it needed.

"The last time we did it, several of them came apart in our hands," she said, "Such a pity, as they were so lovely. The dear late mistress hated to part with them. *Just one more year,* she used to say, and then after she died, no one had the heart to change a thing."

Not for nothing had Trixie run her Uncle Leonard's London home for many years. She had warmed immediately to this old house, responding to its sense of comfort, though she could see it needed refurbishment. She picked up the edge of one of the bed hangings and gently unpicked the rotting thread that held the hem. As she unfolded it, the fabric that had been protected from the light glowed with jewel colors.

"Look," she said. "Here we can see what it used to look like. When I return to London I'll go to the various warehouses to see if something similar may be found. I arranged for those in Uncle Leonard's home to be replaced not very long ago. But it would be a pity to replace these with something completely different, as we did there. This house demands continuity."

Margarethe looked at her in astonishment. She would never have imagined Trixie could know about such things as bed hangings. The housekeeper was even more impressed. In her fashionable gown, delicate slippers and elegant coiffure, Lady Beatrix did not look anything of a housekeeper. And the fact she had the sensitivity to understand that things should not be changed, but simply renewed, warmed Mrs. Truly's heart to her.

After telling the ladies that dinner was customarily served at six, but that today it would be an hour later to allow them time to rest a little and change, Mrs. Truly took herself off. She later told her bosom-bow the cook that Mr. Lukas had chosen well. His betrothed might look like a flibberty-gibbet, but she was not.

From the start, Trixie was treated as the mistress of the house. In the dining room, she was placed at one end of the long refectory-style table with the Baron at the other. Margarethe and Hettie sat opposite each other in the middle, Hettie having again been persuaded she was there as a family member, not a servant.

Lukas was more relaxed than Trixie had ever seen him. He seemed to fit the place, and often talked about his childhood there. "It's been years since I dined in here," said Lukas that first night, looking around the dining room, at the ochre-colored walls hung with dark paintings of dead game birds and hunting scenes. "It was too large for me alone and I couldn't see the point of making fires in here just for me to eat my dinner. But many happy meals have been eaten here. My grandmother used to like to invite the neighbors and often had large parties. It was one of the proudest moments of my life when I was fifteen and deemed old enough to dine with company. I stayed with the gentlemen when the ladies left. My grandfather even poured me a glass of port. I was too overawed to open my mouth, and I can't say I understood everything that was said, but I found it marvelous! It was a real rite of passage."

"I started being hostess at my uncle's table at about the same age," said Trixie. "At least, most of the time. Occasionally he would say the company wasn't suitable and send me upstairs. That didn't please me much, and one time I crept down to see what they were doing. But there were only four of them and they were all sitting very close with their heads together, so I couldn't hear anything. I saw my uncle put his arm around one of the other men, but that's all. I went back to bed."

"You never mentioned that to me before, my dear," said Hettie.

"No, I thought you'd be vexed with me for going down, and then I forgot all about it till now."

Chapter Thirty-Eight

Over the course of the next week, Lukas, with Juno at his heels, took Trixie and Margarethe over the estate. Hettie said she found the wind too sharp and that was understandable, for it soon became clear why Chorley House had been built in the middle of a knot of trees. As soon as they left the protection they afforded, they felt the almost constant wind across the plain.

Trixie was amazed to see how this part of the English countryside differed from what she knew. She was used to gently rolling hills, large white cattle, and wide fields of wheat. Here, they saw flocks of curly-horned sheep cropping the plain. The estate grew wheat and other crops, too, of course. Men and animals could not have survived otherwise.

Lukas was in his element. He explained the field rotation system, and if, by the end of it, although Trixie could still barely distinguish one crop from another, she did learn to recognize a Wiltshire Horn sheep. Lukas told them it was a native short wool animal descended from the large, white sheep that had grazed on Salisbury Plain for centuries. They were bred to withstand the bleak weather. The chief problem now was not the cold, but the foxes, especially in lambing season. For that reason, the shepherds were in the habit of using fox traps. They would place them in areas where fox droppings were found close to the pens, because foxes were known to use the same latrine area repeatedly.

Trixie found his knowledge of it all fascinating and her respect for him grew. Up till then, the gentlemen she had known had all been town bred. While they had a great deal of address, they usually talked of light, entertaining matters, often quite nonsensical, presumably because they thought that was suitable for feminine ears. Lukas treated her as an intellectual equal.

For his part, Lukas began to see the full force of Trixie's charm. The tenants and estate workers took to her immediately. She had little experience of children, but she instinctively bent down to talk to them and made them laugh with silly remarks. She admired the babies, and though she had never been faced with any problem in providing for her uncle and the household in London, commiserated with the wives when they talked of the difficulty of feeding growing sons. A lovely lady, they declared her. A perfect choice for the master. He was inclined to be a bit stiff, but she would soften him up.

On one of these rides Lukas stopped by the farm now tenanted by the ex-Private Potter. When he rapped on the door with the handle of his cane, it was opened by a comely round-cheeked woman with a child of about three who looked at their visitor with intelligent curiosity. When she saw who it was, she grasped his hand and kissed it.

"Oh, sir!" she said, "I'm that glad to see you!" She spoke with a soft west-country burr. "When my Alf come home and told me what you'd a-done for him, and him all set to rob you, I fell to my knees and thanked God for you. You run and fetch your Da, Alfie, he's seeing to the pig."

While the lady of the house urged Lukas and the two ladies into the parlor, offering them tea, the child trotted off and soon returned with his father. Juno gave a low growl when she saw him.

"Now, Juno," said Lukas, his hand on her head, "He's a friend."

Potter had whipped off his cap and, with a sidelong look at Juno, who still manifestly didn't trust him, held out his hand to Lukas. "I hope my wife has made you welcome, sir. We owe you more than we can ever repay. Do you bring out that bit of tansy wine, now, Dolly!"

"And there's me forgetting we had any left!"

She bustled off, in spite of the visitors trying to stop her. She came back with a bottle of a dark liquid, three sturdy drinking glasses and two teacups on a wooden board. She poured a small amount into the three glasses and a thimbleful into the teacups. Then she offered the glasses to the visitors, and she and her husband took the teacups.

Trixie promptly took one and Margarethe, after a little hesitation, followed suit. Lukas picked up the third, and holding it up said, "Here's good health to you and your family, Potter!"

"And to yours, sir, and to yours," responded Potter. "I take this lady," said Potter, indicating Trixie, "to be your future Missus. This other lady must be your sister, seeing as how you're so alike. Well, we wish you as happy as we are." He patted his wife's midsection. "And as lucky with the little 'uns. Our Alfie's the brightest spark you ever met, and we don't expect any less from the second."

They all drank. The wine was very pleasant, with an unusual aromatic flavor.

There was a silence until Trixie broke it. "This is delicious!" she said. The others murmured agreement.

"Dolly makes this in the summer," said Potter. "Her family's been doing it for years. We got here too late, this year, o'course, but next year we'll be sure to save some for you."

"Thank you," said Lukas, putting down his glass. The ladies followed suit. "We must be off. Thank you, Mrs. Potter."

He gave a slight bow. Mrs. Potter blushed rosily and bobbed a curtsey. "You will always be welcome, sir. And know you that the Potter family will do whatever we can for you till our dying breath."

He gave her one of his rare smiles and ushered his ladies outside and into the gig, Juno following behind. He and Potter exchanged a few remarks about farming, and then Lukas climbed in and clicked up the horse.

Margarethe turned to him as soon as they were out of earshot. "What was that about him trying to rob you?"

"Oh, nothing much, really. Poor fellow took to being a rather ineffective highwayman when he came out of the army and could find no work to support his family. Juno saw him off, as a matter of fact. That's why she growled when she saw him. But it was all settled. We got to talking and I offered him the farm."

Both ladies thought there was more to the story than that, but Lukas shook his head. "He's a farmer. That's all anyone needs to know. We don't need to judge a man by what he may have done when he was pushed to it, but by what he does now."

Trixie thought about that all the way home. *Is that how she should think about Lukas?* she wondered.

Chapter Thirty-Nine

Lukas was wondering too. He saw his tenants responding to Trixie. He saw Margarethe blooming in her presence. He saw Mrs. Truly consulting her about the household. He'd realized during the abortive trip to Hatfield that she wasn't the silly girl he had taken her for. But now he found himself thinking of her altogether differently.

Word soon spread that the master of Chorley was back, this time with his fiancée, and the neighboring squires and gentry came to leave cards or spend the prescribed twenty minutes to meet her. They were invited to dinners and card parties, to teas and to suppers. The ladies admired her London wardrobe and the gentlemen admired her figure. "Charming girl," was the general opinion.

Conscious of the need to invite where one had been invited, when no one else mentioned it, Trixie suggested a dinner party. Nothing too formal, the sort of thing she had frequently hosted with her uncle. There would be card tables for guests who wished to play, and billiards were always available. To Margarethe's delight, there was a pianoforte in the drawing room. Her grandmother had believed no home was complete without one. Knowing he would be bringing his sister to stay there, Lukas had given orders for it to be tuned, and Margarethe played every day. She agreed to perform at the party as she had in London. "But only if you sing with me, Trixie," she said.

Trixie and Mrs. Truly examined an old book entitled *Diary and Receipt Book* kept by Lukas's grandmother, in which she described what she had served and when. It was a treasure trove, with menus and recipes going back nearly fifty years. There was also advice on dealing with common complaints such as dandruff and earache, along with methods of cooking all sorts of things. Some of it was age-spotted, very hard to read, and even quite funny.

Take a Pnt of vinegar and boil with honey. Pour over
cut cucumbers and keep cold. V.gd to eat but
exceeding windy.

"I don't think we'll serve that," laughed Trixie. I don't want wind-filled visitors in the drawing room!"

They found a perfect winter menu and copied it: mutton with redcurrant jelly, roasted potatoes and onions, carp collops fried in butter, salsify in cream, and chestnut purée, to end with apple cakes and preserved plums. The retractable leaves at the end of the long dining table were pulled out and they sat thirty people to dinner.

The evening was a great success, due chiefly to Trixie's ability to put everyone at ease. Lukas was welcoming but very dignified and Margarethe, as always, quiet and a little shy. Trixie greeted all the visitors, remembering most of their names, commiserating with the ladies over the difficulty of maintaining any sort of coiffure in the constant wind (not caused by cucumbers, thankfully!) and shamelessly flirting with all the older gentlemen.

The house had been cleaned till it shone and the old oak furniture glowed. Still, there was no denying the dilapidated state of the coverings. When she saw a couple of the ladies raising their eyes at it, she laughed in a voice loud enough for everyone to hear, "Yes, some of the cushions are positively in threads! We shall be refurbishing them, of course, but of a winter evening with the candles and the fire, I must say they look positively *gothick*. It gives one quite a delightful shiver, don't you think?"

Several people agreed and looked around half-laughing as if expecting to see a ghost coming through the paneled walls. After that, no one said anything about the furnishings. Lukas caught her eye and smiled in appreciation.

This was Trixie's element. She knew she was liked and admired here. The memory of those difficult days in London and the Earl's harsh criticism of her behavior was pushed to the back of her mind. When the gentlemen came into the drawing room after their port, she quickly found who wished to play cards, who preferred billiards and who were happy to listen to the musical entertainment. Margarethe played and they both sang. As before, their songs were lighthearted and well known. Many of the visitors joined in.

Lukas looked at his sister laughing at something Trixie said. He saw now that the influence Trixie had on his sister was wholly benign. If only he had understood that before! He was ashamed of the accusations he had hurled at her head the first time they met. And the two made a pretty picture, with Margarethe's fair head next to Trixie's dark curls. He was not the only one to notice it.

"By Jove," said one older gentleman, "You've brought both business and beauty to the place. All you need now is a few young'uns and a husband for that pretty sister of yours, and we'll have you fixed in Wiltshire for sure. And very welcome you'll be!"

He wrung Lukas's hand before returning to the pianoforte to flirt in his ponderous way with Trixie.

When all the guests had finally departed, the three collapsed into the drawing room chairs and looked at each other.

"Oh, it was such fun!" said Margarethe, "You see, Lukas, Trixie is really good at parties. Everyone loves her."

Yes, he did see. And the everyone was beginning to include him.

Chapter Forty

Margarethe repeated more than once her desire to go back to Stonehenge, but her brother had replied mysteriously that they had to wait for the right day. As the weeks passed, she stopped asking. Trixie thought Lukas didn't want to go for some reason and was simply leading his sister along. It didn't really seem to accord with his character, though, and she was surprised.

Then, on the 21st of December, Lukas announced that late the following afternoon they would be going for a drive.

"Why? It will be freezing by then! Why not earlier?" exclaimed Margarethe. "Where are we going?"

"You'll see," was all he would say.

The following afternoon, loaded into a carriage with hot bricks at their feet and covered in heavy blankets, they set out, back in the direction they had come from London.

They had not gone far before the drivers reined in. "The dog's behind us, sir," said the driver when Lukas asked what the problem was.

Sure enough, there was Juno, trotting along behind them, her tongue hanging out. Lukas sighed and opened the carriage door. "I didn't think you'd enjoy being out in the cold, but come in then, you silly animal," he said, his smile belying his words.

Juno scrambled up and collapsed on their feet.

Trixie patted her head. "She's determined never to be left again," she said fondly. "If she sees a carriage leaving with her favorite person in it, she's bound and determined to be in the carriage too."

"I would say it's a question as to who her favorite person is." Lukas looked at Juno who had her eyes closed in bliss as Trixie scratched her behind the ears. They all laughed when Trixie stopped and Juno looked at her in reproach before bumping under her hand with her muzzle to make her continue.

"I cannot believe you are making us do this!" said Margarethe, a while later. "It's absolutely freezing!" She huddled into the blankets. "I wish you'd say where we're going. Why did we start out when the daylight's almost over? It makes no sense!"

But Lukas refused to be drawn, merely shaking his head and smiling at their confusion. It wasn't until they left the main road and began bumping up a narrow path that they realized they were going to Stonehenge. And they were not alone. People were converging on the place on foot, on horseback and in farm carts.

The carriage drew to a halt and they all descended. Juno trotting behind them, they walked into the broken circle of enormous stones. There they could see there were several flat tablets lying in the grass. His hand on the dog's head, Lukas urged the two women up on to the tallest of them and told them to turn to the west. They stood there, shivering, even with coats and cloaks and shawls and scarves. The huge stones seemed to hum in the wind, towering around them like eyeless giants, and the chill of the stone beneath their feet penetrated the soles of their boots.

A weak sun had shone all day in the pale winter sky. Now, as they watched, it sank lower and lower until it stood directly between the two western pillars of stone and shone between them into the center of the circle.

A collective "Ah!" arose from the people gathered there. Trixie and Margarethe forgot all about the cold.

"It's a miracle!" said Margarethe, entranced.

"Nay, lass," said a farmer beside her. "It's showing us that folks who came before us knew what they was doing when they put up these here stones. Like a church it is, a church in a field."

"It's the winter solstice today," said Lukas, "the day when there is the least daylight. The stones are arranged so the setting sun shines between them. On the day of the summer solstice, with the longest daylight, it shines at sunrise through the east-facing stones over there." He indicated a stone doorway behind them.

They watched in silence till the sky was completely dark, then Margarethe threw her arms around Lukas's neck.

"Thank you, Lukas! Thank you! I've never seen anything so wonderful. May we come back for the summer solstice?"

"If we're here then, by all means. We used to come here for picnics in the summer when I was a boy. As cold as they are now, the stones retain the heat of the sun. It's lovely to lie on those flat tablets with the warm in your back and look up at the sky."

"Oh, we'll be here, won't we?"

"I hope so," replied Lukas. "It depends on Trixie." He looked towards her.

"I... I don't know," said Trixie, glad it was too dark for him to see the expression on her face.

As they returned to the carriage, they walked in silence, not knowing what to say next.

Juno ran back and forth, snuffling in the grass where the scent of rabbits, long since snug in their burrows, interested her much more than the setting sun. *I don't know what all the fuss was about,* she said to herself. *But I do want my dinner.*

Chapter Forty-One

The day after the trip to Stonehenge, Lukas excused himself, saying he had to see the estate manager and left immediately after breakfast. Trixie spent the morning with Mrs. Truly examining the linen cupboards and taking note of items that needed replacing. Hettie, who was what she called a *good plain seamstress,* had undertaken to repair anything that needed it. She was glad, she said, to have something to do that didn't require being on her feet all day, and provided she had good working candles, could see perfectly well, thank God.

Trixie had a certain amount of linen that came to her from her mother. It was embroidered with C, for her mother's family name: Carruthers. It was kept in a large chest in her bedroom. She and Hettie had carefully shaken it out every year and placed sachets of cloves and lavender in its folds. Now she wondered if it should be brought here. Or would it go to the London house?

These details of married life had never occurred to her before. In truth, the reality of marriage had not really been in her mind at all until arriving here. She had just been considering it an inevitable event, in a vague and distant future. Margarethe's question about whether they would be here in the summer had caught her unprepared. Now it occupied her totally, not the little things, like sheets and dinner services — she had just remembered she had a whole set of that from her mother, too — but the reality of living with this man she knew she loved. Did he want her too? She was conscious of a change in his attitude towards her. Was he still marrying her only as a matter of honor? What did his comment at Stonehenge really mean? Should she say something? What?

Determined to put these jumbled thoughts out of her head, she decided to go for a gallop. She loved riding and it had always been the surest way clearing her mind. She was alone that afternoon. Margarethe was off on some mysterious project of her own, and Lukas was still out.

She had not brought her own saddle horse, not wishing to impose the expense of feeding it upon her host, and thinking that in all probability the ground would be too hard for riding. She regretted it now, for though the wind was chill and the days cold, it was fine for the time of year.

She changed into her riding habit, with its voluminous skirts and tight waisted jacket, put a warm cloak over her shoulders and walked to the stables.

"No, m'lady," said the head groom when asked. "We don't have a lady's horse no more, the mistress being gone so long, God rest her soul. Fact is, at the moment there's only the carriage horses, and the master's hunter. He's took Betsy with the gig being as the dog won't stay home without him, and the other two saddle horses are at the Smithy. Sorry."

Trixie looked at Zeus, Lukas's big hunter. He was a large beast, but she knew he was well trained. "Then I'll take Zeus," she said decisively.

"He's too big for you, m'lady!" The groom was horrified. "I wouldn't be easy in my mind letting you take him."

"You are not letting me take him. You are following my orders. I'm telling you to put a lady's saddle on him. At once." Trixie was at her most imperious.

"But...."

"But nothing. Do as I say."

Anyone who knew Trixie knew that the surest way to make her do something was to say she could not. By now she was determined to ride Zeus, come what may.

Reluctantly, the groom found a lady's saddle, deliberately taking his time over it. Then when Trixie was helped onto the block to mount the animal it was found to be too low, and more time was taken finding something to put on top that she could step onto. By the time she was mounted, the stirrup lengthened, as she was taller than Lukas's grandmother had been, and ready to go, the afternoon was half gone.

As she rode out of the yard, she was conscious of her heart beating in her ears, for she was further from the ground than she had ever been before, and the animal seemed even larger now she was atop him. Nevertheless, she held her head high, kept the reins steady and as she reached the driveway leading away from the house, kicked the horse into a trot, then a canter.

Zeus was well trained and responded to her slightest command. She calmed down. This was fun! She urged him into a gallop. They flew through the junipers and were just coming to the lane that led to the main road when she saw the gig coming towards her. She saw it draw to a halt and Lukas stand up on the driving board, but that's all she saw. The big horse carried her by in a flash and if Lukas shouted, she didn't hear it.

Exhilarated, she continued up past the pens of sheep, past the fields of wheat or turnip, or whatever they were, and arrived at the main road. She drew the horse back into a canter and turned left, away from the way to Stonehenge. She remembered from their rides with Lukas that there was a turning up the road that led to open pasture. She could gallop to her heart's content.

This she did. She let Zeus have his head. He seemed to enjoy it as much as she, for he covered mile after mile without seeming to want to stop. The sun sank lower and lower in the sky until it hit Trixie full in the eyes and she realized with a start she would be lucky to get home while it was still light. She drew the horse into a canter, turned him in a wide arc and began back.

She knew that if she went east, away from the setting sun, she would find her way home. But it was further than she thought. It was some time before she found the path she had taken to reach the open land, and it was fully dark by the time she cantered through the juniper wood up to Chorley House.

Lukas was standing at the bottom of the steps with Juno by his side. The flambeaux had been lit and she could see by their light that his face was set and furious.

"Get down immediately!" he said.

"I would, if you would help me. It's too far without a block," she replied, keeping her voice light.

Without a word, he stepped forward. She took her foot out of the stirrup, lifted her leg gracefully over the pommel, let go of the reins and slid into his arms. He held her for a moment at his eye level. She thought he might be going to kiss her, but when he spoke, his voice was cold.

"Dammit, Trixie," he said. "Just when I thought you could be trusted."

He let her slide to her feet. She found she was shaking, and she had to clasp his arm.

"Wh... what do you mean?" she said.

"Be trusted to have a modicum of self-control! I understand from Smithers you insisted on taking Zeus, even though he tried to stop you. That's the trouble with you, Trixie! When you get an idea in your head, you don't stop to think! Look at you, you're shaking. You could have been killed."

He had raised his voice by the end of this declaration. Juno looked up at him enquiringly and then went to stand next to Trixie. She patted her head distractedly.

"I'm not shaking because of that, or at least, not because I was afraid. I wasn't! Not a bit! My legs and arms are tired, that's all. Zeus was a perfect gentleman. I could ride him any day."

"You will not ride him any day, or ever again," said Lukas. "I utterly forbid it. He is too much horse for you!"

"No he isn't! We had a fine time. He enjoyed it and so did I!" Trixie's dander was up now, and she didn't know what she was saying. "But that's it, isn't it?" she said hotly, "Just because you don't like to have fun, you don't think anyone else should."

"That's ridiculous!" Lukas shot back. "What you did was dangerous and you know it! You don't know the country! He could have stumbled in a rabbit hole, you could have fallen off miles away and we wouldn't have been able to find you in the dark. You could have died of cold."

"Oh!" Trixie stamped her foot. "Could have, could have, if you live your life by could haves you would never do anything! I refuse to be like that! Now let me by, I want to take this wonderful horse back to the stable."

"You will go indoors. I'll do it."

"Stop telling me what to do!" Trixie was shouting now. "I'm not married to you yet, thank God, and after this I never shall be! I will not live with a man who wants to control what I think and what I do! Consider our betrothal at an end! Now let me go, I say."

Lukas drew in his breath as if to say something, but then let it out again. "Very well, do as you please."

He turned to walk up the steps into the house then stopped.

"Heel, Juno," he said curtly.

But Juno looked from him to Trixie and stayed where she was.

"Stay there then, you foolish animal," said Lukas under his breath, and continued up the steps.

Trixie, blinking back the tears that came to her eyes, knelt down and put her face against the dog's muzzle. "Thank you, Juno," she whispered.

Then she stood up and led Zeus towards the stables. Juno, trotting alongside, was glad they were putting this horse back where he belonged. Everyone knew horses were a damned nuisance.

Chapter Forty-Two

The next day was Christmas Eve, but Trixie had never felt less like celebrating. To avoid seeing Lukas again, she had taken her dinner in her room the night before and had snuffed the candles, pretending to be asleep when both Margarethe and Hettie came tapping at her door. That morning she came down late for breakfast hoping she had missed him.

She had. Only Margarethe was there, drinking a cup of tea and looking as pleased with herself as someone of her retiring disposition could.

"Good morning!" she said solicitously when Trixie appeared, "Are you feeling better this morning? Lukas said you were tired from your horse ride yesterday afternoon. Did you really take Zeus? I can't believe it! I would have been terrified! I came up see you after dinner but you were already asleep."

"Yes, thank you. I feel much better." But her words were belied by her hollow-eyed appearance and Margarethe looked doubtful.

"Perhaps you should have a lie-down this afternoon. We dine early, you know, because of church later."

The prospect of going to church and seeing all the neighbors was far from pleasant, but Trixie knew she should go. Her absence would be remarked upon and might give rise to nosy visits of enquiry after her health. She was planning on returning to London as soon as her uncle could send a carriage for her. She would write him a note today.

Margarethe was once again involved in some business of her own and Lukas, thankfully, remained out of sight. Juno was quite the opposite. She stuck to her side as never before. She had apparently slept outside her door, for when the maids brought in her tea and hot water that morning, she heard them scolding her for being in the way.

"Get on out of there, you silly animal!" she heard one of them say. "I nearly dropped this jug o' hot water all over you. Serve you right if I did!"

But Juno was still there when she left her room to go down for breakfast and hadn't left her since. When she walked over to the stables to give Zeus an apple for being such a gentleman the day before, Juno trotted along beside her, when she went down to the kitchen to see if things were ready for the meals over the holidays she went with her, and it was testimony to her loyalty that when she left, Juno left too. Normally she would have stayed there, getting under Cook's feet until she fed her a few scraps.

Then, when Trixie did go up to her room in the afternoon, not to lie down but to wrap the gifts she had brought with her, she lay outside her door until she opened it and invited her in. The dog had been strictly forbidden in any but the master's bedchamber before, and now looked at her doubtfully.

"You can come in, Juno," said Trixie. "The way I'm going, it may only ever be we ladies in my bedroom!"

She padded in and lay down by the desk where Trixie was wrapping the gifts.

She had bought shawls for Margarethe and Hettie and had pondered long and hard over what to give Lukas. In the end she bought him a silver rimmed quizzing glass on a black ribbon. Most of the gentlemen she knew wore one, but he didn't. Perhaps he didn't like them, but she didn't know what else to offer. Really, she didn't know his tastes at all. She wrapped everything in silk paper and tied the parcels with ribbon. Then she lay down on her bed. Perhaps she *was* a little tired.

She awoke to the sound of her maid tapping on her door and Juno trotting over to it.

"Being as you didn't ring, I left it as long as I could," said the maid, "but it's getting late. Dinner will be served shortly. We've already had ours, so's we can get ready for church while you are having yours."

"Of course, I don't know why I slept so long." Trixie shook the sleep from her head. She really did feel much better. "My red velvet, don't you think? For Christmas Eve?"

She may have made the choice to remain a spinster all her life, she reasoned, and she would be leaving as soon as she could, but no reason why she shouldn't look her best. Let him see she didn't care.

So when Trixie descended the wide staircase, the ever-faithful Juno by her side, she looked glorious. Her ruby red velvet gown had a wide froth of lace at the bosom and cuffs. She wore her mother's pearls, and her dark hair was brushed till it shone then gathered up into a topknot, with loose curls falling to her ears.

She had the satisfaction of seeing Lukas's eyes widen as she came into the drawing room, but all he said was "Good evening, Beatrix."

So he was back with *Beatrix* was he? *Trixie* was no more. So be it.

"Good evening Baron," she replied with even more formality. She was still angry with him, but she couldn't deny he looked magnificent. His royal blue coat fit his broad shoulders like a glove and reflected the intense blue of his eyes. His neck cloth lay in perfect folds, and his blond hair curled over his forehead in a natural disarray it took most men hours to achieve. His buff colored pantaloons were perfectly smooth, and the surface of his Hessian boots was like glass. She had to drag her eyes away from him.

She went to sit next to Margarethe, who looked lovely. Trixie had been with her when she had chosen the gown she now wore. It was of a delicate pale pink silk with a shimmering white underdress. They had visited the Pantheon Bazaar and Trixie had persuaded her to buy a delicate shell necklace which complemented the gown to perfection. Her flaxen hair was, as usual, done up in complicated braids.

"Margarethe," she cried, "You look like an angel!"

"And you look as if you have stepped right out of a London salon! The neighbors will never have seen anyone so fashionable. What an odd assortment we are!"

Yes an angel and the devil, thought Lukas. But he simply remarked, "you both look very nice."

He was even more confused by his feelings for Trixie. He couldn't help being drawn to her, and he recognized her admirable qualities, but her disregard for convention deeply disturbed him. He wasn't sure whether he was angry because she'd come to no harm on his hunter, or angry because he wished she had. Nothing too serious, of course, just enough to teach her a lesson.

Chapter Forty-Three

As they walked to the family pew, Lukas and his ladies made quite a stir. They were an exceedingly handsome group, but, as everyone afterwards agreed, not too high to acknowledge their acquaintances and smile at their neighbors. Trixie found peace in listening to the well-known words of the Christmas Service and told herself she could face the next few days with equanimity. Then she would be gone.

She was surprised when Margarethe engaged the vicar in conversation after the service, seeming to enumerate one by one the differences in the service from the ones she was accustomed to. Lukas was plainly surprised too, and finally had to tap her on the shoulder with an apology, to remind her that the horses should not be kept waiting in the cold.

The reason for the delay became clear as they entered the hall of Chorley House. The normal candles had been extinguished, and in their place a tree glowed in the center with a myriad of small tapers. The scent was lovely: wintry and fresh.

"This is what we do at home," said Margarethe. "A Christmas tree. I wanted it to be a surprise!"

A juniper tree about six feet tall was strung with garlands of red berries. They made a lovely contrast with the juniper's own black berries. Cut-down tapers had been fixed by hot wax to clothes pegs and pinned to the branches.

"We have special wooden clips for the candles at home, but this was the best I could think of."

"So that's what you've been doing these last few days!" Trixie marveled. "It's wonderful! I've never seen a Christmas tree before! You are clever, Margarethe!"

"Yes, indeed," said Lukas, and squeezed her hand. "Thank you, Grete. It is a wonderful memory of our other home."

All the servants who had not returned home for Christmas came into the hall, exclaiming at the sight. Margarethe took her brother's hand and said "Sing with me, Lukas."

Together they sang,

> O Tannenbaum, o Tannenbaum,
> wie treu sind deine Blätter!

Margarethe's light soprano and Lukas's tuneful baritone produced a charming effect. All the listeners clapped and begged for more.

"Let us sing some English Christmas songs," said Margarethe. "Then you can all join in."

So the assembled company sang *Oh, Come All Ye Faithful*, *Hark the Herald Angels Sing*, *God Rest Ye Merry Gentlemen*, and, given the local agriculture, the one closest to their hearts, *While Shepherds Watched Their Flocks By Night*.

Trixie was at first surprised that Lukas knew all these carols and sang them with his lusty baritone, but then remembered he had spent many Christmases here with his grandparents. She sighed. There was so much admirable about this man!

They had a cold supper in the breakfast room, which Trixie explained was what they always did at home, to give the staff as little work as possible.

"I thought we should give them leave to go home for Christmas. That's what we do in London. And we give them a Christmas Box. Not a box, really, a few shillings extra. I asked Mrs. Truly to talk to you about all that, Lukas."

"She did and it was all arranged."

He was irritated he hadn't thought of it himself, especially now he knew it had been Trixie's idea. It was more convenient for him to think of her as entirely self-centered.

"At home we give each other little gifts on Christmas Eve," said Margarethe sensing his annoyance and to change the subject. I have a trifle for each of you. Perhaps we can do that after supper in the drawing room."

"Oh, we usually do it on Christmas Day," said Trixie, but it's a nice idea. Let's."

So after supper they exchanged presents. Margarethe and Hettie were delighted with their silk shawls, Hettie protesting that the gift was too costly, but wrapping her thin shoulders in it with a frisson of pleasure. Lukas seemed surprised to receive anything at all from her, and even more surprised when he saw what it was.

"I've been meaning to get one of these," he said, "but never got around to it. Thank you, Beatrix." He put the ribbon under one of the buttons on his waistcoat and slipped it into the watch pocket. He gave her a smile. Not the full glorious smile he was capable of, but a smile.

Margarethe gave her brother a pair of gloves, explaining she'd had the size copied from an old pair. To Hettie she gave a lace collar, and to Trixie an amber necklace she had found at the Pantheon Bazaar.

"I thought it might look good with your new gown," she said.

Trixie thanked her very much, though she thought after her shaming experience when she wore it last, she would never put that gown on again.

Hettie gave them all beautifully hemmed handkerchiefs and then Lukas produced his offerings. A new atlas for Hettie, who received it with gasps of delight, for his sister, a beautifully illustrated book of classical statuary, including the Elgin Marbles, and for Trixie a gold-edged diary.

"With all the social events you attend, I thought it might be useful," he said.

She thanked him. *Just like him*, she thought. *Practical and impersonal.*

Chapter Forty-Four

Christmas day was very quiet. They rose late after tea and toast in bed, ate a cold nuncheon in the breakfast room. They decided against a walk in the afternoon as it was coming on to freezing rain. Hettie and Margarethe were delighted to spend the time by the fire reading their new books, Hettie exclaiming over the illustrations of far-flung places and people with which the atlas was embellished.

"Just look at these Chinese!" she exclaimed. "All their clothing is covered in the most wonderful embroidery!" Then a little later, "It says here that the Hindu believe we are all reincarnated in an eternal cycle. Well!" She put the book down. "If I am to be reincarnated, I wish to come back here, with you, Trixie and you Margarethe, and the Baron, for I do not believe there can be a better place on the earth than here with you. And Juno, of course."

She looked fondly at the dog who, since Trixie was in the room, was in her accustomed position in front of the fire. She flopped her tail when she heard her name but otherwise didn't move.

"Where's my shawl?" said Trixie suddenly. "I'm sure I took it off earlier when I got a little warm by the fire."

She looked all around, then got up. Juno immediately did the same. They walked together into the breakfast room, to see if she had left it there. She had not.

"Where's my shawl, Juno?" asked Trixie.

But if the dog knew, she wasn't saying.

They wandered back to the drawing room, Trixie retracing her steps that afternoon in her mind. She was sure she'd had it until after lunch. She sat down again, shaking her head.

A little while later, Lukas came into the room, carrying her shawl.

"This was on my chair in the study," he said. "It's yours, isn't it, Beatrix? Did you want something in there?"

"No," she replied, furrowing her brow. "I wouldn't go in there without your invitation. And I certainly would not have left anything on your chair."

Lukas handed her the shawl. "You may use my chair any time you like, I hope you know that."

After her ungracious words to him, his response was almost a caress. Trixie didn't know what to say, so said nothing. He went to the fire and threw on more logs.

"I'll be glad when the full complement of servants is back," he said. "I never realized what a job it is keeping all these fires burning."

On Boxing Day the weather continued the same, with freezing rain on and off all day. Margarethe was learning a new piece on the piano. Hettie was still engrossed in her atlas, wrapped in a wool shawl on top of her silk one, which it seemed she would never take off.

Trixie had been working on an acrostic poem, with which she hoped to stump Hettie, who was a master at them. It was a game they'd played for years. It was hard, as she had decided to use both the first and the last word of the line, which meant finding two lots of words with first letters that spelled out things when read downwards, but also rhymed when read normally. She had used several sheets of paper with her efforts and they lay discarded on the floor.

As she picked up her last effort to carry on with it, she saw Lukas's new quizzing glass under it. Mystified, she picked it up.

"What's this doing here?" she wondered out loud.

Her companions disclaimed all knowledge, so she got up and went looking for Lukas. Had he decided he didn't want it? Surely he wouldn't have just put it on the floor next to her like that. She knew he wasn't that ungentlemanly.

With Juno next to her, she met him coming down the stairs.

"So there it is!" he said, looking at his quizzing glass in her hand. "Did you need it for something?"

"No, I found it under some papers I was working on. I thought you'd put it there."

"Why would I do that?"

"I don't know... I thought perhaps you didn't want it."

"Of course I want it! And even if I didn't, do you think I'd be so ungrateful as to leave it like that? You obviously have a very poor opinion of me, Beatrix."

"Oh, stop calling me Beatrix!" said Trixie crossly. "And I don't have a poor opinion of you. Not that poor, anyway!"

"That's a relief, at least," he said with a smile. "A slightly poor opinion I can live with. And I'll stop calling you Beatrix if you stop calling me Baron."

"Very well... Lukas. Here." She thrust the glass at him.

"Thank you. I took it off because there was a knot in the ribbon. I put it down in my room. I remembered it just now and went to get it. It was gone."

"Perhaps one of the servants found it and then dropped it in the drawing room."

"Seems most unlikely. Anyway, no harm done. In fact, maybe some good. That's the longest conversation we've had in nearly a week."

They looked at each other for a moment. Juno looked up at both of them. Trixie found herself blushing. "I'll get back to what I was doing," she said, and left him.

Chapter Forty-Five

Trixie knew she should write to her uncle about sending a carriage for her. By the time her letter arrived he would be home from Lady March's. The following afternoon she sat down at the escritoire in her bedchamber to write, but found herself unable to do it. If she went home to London she would be burning her bridges. The Earl would certainly carry out his threat of taking her to Shelby Place and more or less imprisoning her there. Is that what she wanted? She threw her pen down in frustration.

"What shall I do, Juno?" she said. The dog was, as usual, in front of her fire. "I don't want to go but I can't stay!"

In response she got up and came over to put her muzzle in Trixie's lap. She gently pulled her silky ears. Then she looked out the window. It had stopped raining. In fact, a weak sun was shining. She would take a walk. That would help to clear her head and make a decision.

She put on her boots then her pelisse and heavy cloak with the hood she could tie beneath her chin, and looked for her gloves. She found one of them but not the other. She was sure she'd put them both on the chair after church on Christmas Eve. That was the last time she'd been out.

She looked all around but could not find the other glove. "Where is it?" she asked out loud. Juno ran to the door expectantly.

"Good idea," she said. "Let's ask Prewitt."

"No, my lady," he said, when they found him in the hall. "And in any case, I must discourage you from going out. It's going to rain again soon."

"But the sun is shining!"

"Yes, but if you go upstairs and look out the top windows over the trees, you will see clouds gathering in the east. Those always bring cold rain or even snow. I wish you would not go."

At that moment, Lukas emerged from the study.

"I thought I heard your voice," he said. "I believe this is yours."

He handed her the missing glove.

"I've been looking for that! Where did you find it?"

"On my chair, just like the shawl."

"How did it get there? I haven't been near the study! I left it in my bedchamber!"

She looked at the glove in puzzlement. "That's the second thing that has mysteriously moved from my possession to yours, my shawl and now my glove."

"And don't forget my glass somehow made its way to you."

They both had the same thought at the same time.

"Juno!" they said, and looked down at her.

In response, she flopped her tail.

"Why on earth are you playing these games?" said Trixie.

"I expect she's just bored," said Lukas. "And it's her idea of fun."

Fun? said Juno to herself, looking at them in turn. *You think it's fun trying to find ways to get you two together?*

"Anyway, Beatrix," continued Lukas, "why are you dressed like that? You're not going out? It's going to rain."

"So Prewitt tells me. But I need a walk. Even if it does rain, I'm not made of sugar and I won't melt."

"Come with me."

Lukas drew her into the study and closed the door.

"I wish you to stay at home," he said coldly. "I know I have no right to forbid you to go, but if I were still your fiancé, I should do so. When it rains on the plain at this time of the year, with all the wind, it is extremely cold. Do not go."

"Then it is just as well we are no longer betrothed," said Trixie, ignoring the second part of Lukas's statement, "because I am going for a walk."

"Lady Beatrix!" Lukas's voice was furious.

"Baron!" Trixie replied in kind.

She turned to the door. "Come Juno," she said.

Looking first at her, then at Lukas, Juno followed, her tail drooping.

Trixie marched to the front door, wrenched it open and stepped outside. Just as she thought. It was really not that cold. The sun was doing its best to shine and there was very little wind. It was about a mile and a half to the other side of the wood. She would just do that and go a little further to look at the sheep, then turn around. She wouldn't be out more than an hour. She set off briskly down the drive to the wood, with Juno zigzagging back and forth, now at her heels, now snuffling off in the bushes.

As she walked she angrily reviewed Lukas's character. She knew his quick temper was probably tied in some way to his dreadful war experiences and she was sorry he had had to live through them, but really! He was insensitive, overbearing and hopelessly old fashioned. *If I were still betrothed to him, he would forbid me! What? To go for a walk? How dare he? Which century does he think we're living in? I suppose he'd lock me in a chastity belt when he went away, too!* Muttering angrily to herself, she stamped her way up the path.

Chapter Forty-Six

She stamped her way right through the woods so intent on her thoughts she did not notice the weather changing. The sun disappeared behind the low clouds and as she emerged from the wood onto the path up to the main road, the wind hit her with all its force. It was coming straight across the plain from the east and hit her hard on her side. There was no way to avoid it. Then it began to sleet, stinging her cheeks and making her eyes water.

"Juno!" she called, meaning to go no further. But there was no answering bark, no sign of the waving tail. Calling "Juno! Juno!" she walked forward, scanning to the left and right through the sleet. There was a sudden break in the clouds and she could make out the sheep pens with the black backs of the sheepdogs guarding them, but no Juno.

Then suddenly, she saw her. A flash of yellow against the dark earth. She ran forward, the wind now behind her, pushing her on. The sky clouded over once more and she had to simply guess where the dog was. She called again, and this time she heard a weak bark, more of a whimper. She ran towards the sound, and found her.

Juno was lying on her side, her left front leg in a pool of blood, caught in the ugly teeth of a fox trap. Trixie fell to her knees and tried to pry the teeth open. It was too strong for her. Anyway, even if she managed to open it, how would she keep it wide while she extricated Juno's leg? Standing up, she looked around. She needed something to pry between the teeth. There were no trees on the field, so she stumbled over to the closest sheep pen, the wind buffeting her and the sleet driving against her body.

The pen was formed by thick branches hammered into the earth, with saplings and thinner branches woven between them. She pulled off the thickest ones she could, paying no attention to her torn gloves and cut palms. Then she stumbled back to Juno and knelt down, forcing a branch between the teeth of the trap. She had to push and pull to do it, and blood oozed from the terrible wound, but Juno bore it all, her trusting eyes on her.

With the sleet driving against her back and the wind lashing at her cloak, she pushed in a slightly thicker branch, removed the first, then another, removing the one before it until the teeth were open enough for her to gently extract the dog's leg. It was cut almost in two, the broken bone white against the torn and bleeding flesh.

She stood up again, and reaching beneath her sodden skirt, tried to tear her petticoat. But her hands were frozen and useless. She took one of the branches and stabbed at the white cotton until it made a hole. Then she forced her stiff fingers into the hole and ripped with all her strength until she finally managed to pull away a strip.

She searched around the icy ground until she found a fairly straight sapling amongst the wood she had torn from the pen. She stood up and placing her boot on one end, managed to snap it in two. Juno lay perfectly still as she manipulated her leg as best she could back into its normal shape, put the pieces of wood on either side of it and wrapped it with the strip of cotton, holding it with her teeth as she pulled it as tight as she could. Still using her teeth, she split the end of the bandage and tied it off.

Then she tried picking up the dog in her arms, but she was too heavy for her. She thought for a moment, then untied her hood and took off her cloak. The driving hail beat on her bare head and drenched her pelisse in moments. She lay the cloak on the ground and half tugged, half rolled Juno onto it. With a superhuman effort, she tied two opposite ends together to make the sort of sling she had seen the countrywomen carry their babies in. She put the loop around her neck, slipped one arm through and stood up. She staggered and almost fell, but with sheer determination, righted herself.

She found she could hardly walk a step with the heavy animal wrapped in the sodden cloak and the freezing rain that was now coming at her full in the face. But she set her chin in a way her Uncle Leonard would have recognized and forced herself to move forward. She tried to think of something else, something that would make her angry enough to forget where she was: Lukas's peremptory demands, his stern face, his unyielding temperament. But all she could remember was his strong arm when he stopped her from falling out of the carriage in Hatfield, and the way he had held her at eye level the other day when she thought he was going to kiss her. Oh, how she wished he were there now. He would carry her and Juno and think nothing of it!

One footstep at a time, she told herself, *just think of one footstep at a time*. Slowly, slowly, she crossed the field to the path, stumbling and falling to her knees more than once, but forcing herself to get up. At last she was on the path towards home. Now the wind blew the sleeting rain against her side, not directly into her face. *One footstep at a time, just one footstep at a time.*

It seemed to take hours, but at last she was in the shelter of the wood. The protection from the buffeting of the wind was immediate, and she stumbled forward, shivering, her tears of relief mixing with the freezing rain on her face. But suddenly she knew she could go no further. Now she was out of the wind, she would lie down, just for a minute. She sank to her knees and then her side, and closed her eyes. She lay there for what could have been five minutes or five hours. Then suddenly, she no longer felt so cold. It fact, she was warm. She wanted to take off her cloak, but found it was weighted down by something and gave up. She imagined she heard the sound of the hoofbeats thudding down the path towards her, and smiled in her warm dream.

Chapter Forty-Seven

It was Lukas on Zeus. He saw her lying on the path with what looked like her cloak bundled in her arms. Leaping down and going to her, he realized the bundle was Juno. Oblivious to the freezing rain, he took off his cloak, removed Juno and the sling from around Trixie's neck and put it around his own, against his back. Then he wrapped Trixie in his cloak and picked her up. Holding her tight against his chest with one arm, he mounted Zeus with the other.

Then they were galloping back towards Chorley House. Trixie's eyelids fluttered and she looked up.

"Lukas!" she said, and closed her eyes again.

When they arrived, Lukas slid off the big hunter.

Prewitt was waiting by the door, with Margarethe, Hettie and Mrs. Truly just inside.

"No questions. Just do as I say," he said, carrying Trixie into the house, with Juno still around his back. "Prewitt, put Juno by the fire in the drawing room and call for Smithers from the stables to come and take a look at her. Mrs. Truly, send someone up to Lady Beatrix's bedchamber with more logs for the fire. Miss Wood, bring tea, warm but not too hot. Grete, come with me."

Lukas carried Trixie up the stairs two at a time. In her bedchamber, he sat her in a chair a little away from the fire, still dazed and only semi-conscious. He turned to his sister.

"Now quickly Grete, take off Trixie's wet things, but do not rub her dry. Pat her gently. Put her in a chemise and blankets. Nothing constricting. And remember, don't rub."

He went downstairs and examined Juno. He quickly understood what had happened and marveled that Trixie had done what she did. She had almost certainly saved the dog's life and hopefully, her leg. When Smithers arrived, Lukas said, "Looks like she was caught in a fox trap. Get a proper splint, some basilicum powder, bandages, and a horse blanket. Take her up to my room by the fire."

Hettie appeared from the kitchen with a tea tray. "I'll take this up to Lady Beatrix, shall I sir?"

"Yes, just make sure it's not hot. Warm but not hot. Give it to Grete and tell her to put a lot of sugar in and feed it by teaspoons to Trixie. Then go and fetch the balm from my shaving things and find some bandages."

"Yes, sir."

Margarethe called down from the top of the stairs. "She's dry and wrapped in blankets, Lukas, but she's shivering dreadfully and seems confused. And her hands are dreadfully cut. Shall I put her to bed?"

"No, Hettie is coming with the tea. Make her drink it, by spoonfuls if necessary. Lots of sugar." Then he raised his voice, "Prewitt, where are those damned logs?"

"Here, sir," said the voice of a maid.

"Take them up and pile them by Lady Beatrix's hearth."

Lukas knelt down to look at Juno, whose eyes were open. The dog gave his hand a dry lick.

He patted the matted head. "You'll be all right. She saved you, you know, at the expense of her own safety." Then he said under his breath, "Oh, Trixie, Trixie, …."

Then he went swiftly up the stairs. Trixie had her eyes closed and her head back against the chair, Margarethe was putting spoonfuls of tea between her lips, and Hettie was waiting with the balm and bandages. She had not attempted to use them. Like everyone else, she was simply obeying Lukas's orders. It never crossed anyone's mind to do otherwise.

"Should I bandage her poor hands, sir?" she said. "Margarethe says they are dreadfully cut."

"Yes, but first let me move her a little further away from the fire. I'm going to build it up and make it very warm in here, but she should not be close to the flames. That's a mistake people make with people suffering from extreme cold. Like making drinks too hot. Too much sudden heat is dangerous. I saw it frequently in Russia."

He picked up Trixie and the chair she was sitting in and placed her on the other side of the room. Then he carefully built up the fire with as many of the logs as it could hold.

By the time Trixie's hands were treated by a tut-tutting Hettie, and all the tea had been drunk, the room was getting very warm. Lukas went to the door. "Thank you, Hettie, Grete," he said. "I shall look after her now. As I said, I've seen cases like this before and I know what is to be done."

The two women looked at each other, but neither said a word. They left, quietly closing the door behind them.

Lukas tore off his coat and undid his waistcoat. Then he ripped open his shirt. He picked Trixie up and sat her down in his lap, her body clad in only the chemise next to his bare chest. Then he wrapped them both firmly in a blanket. She was still dazed and shivering uncontrollably. She looked at him with blank eyes.

They sat like that, their skin touching, as the fire blazed and the room grew ever warmer. After a while, Trixie's shivering stopped. Lukas looked at her anxiously. He felt her bare feet. They were warm. He breathed a sigh of relief, re-wrapped the blankets firmly and sat there holding her as she fell asleep.

Chapter Forty-Eight

When Trixie awoke she did not know where she was. It was dark, the room lit only by the glowing embers of the huge fire. But she felt wonderfully warm and safe. Then as her senses returned, she realized Lukas was holding her. His wonderful scent filled her nostrils, then against her cheek she could feel the muscles in his chest and the fine hair that had so fascinated her that day by the pump in Hatfield. A flood of memory came to her. She remembered Juno being caught in the fox trap, wrapping her in her cloak to carry and being so cold, so cold.

She lifted her head and could see Lukas's shirt was open to his waist. Only the thin cotton of her chemise separated them. She looked up into his face.

"What... why...." She began, then a surge of emotion stopped her. Her breath came in short gasps.

"Trixie!" he said hoarsely, and bent forward to kiss her fiercely on the lips.

She lifted her arms around his neck and, the blankets falling from her almost naked shoulders, returned his embrace with a passion she had never known before.

"But what... why are you...?" she said when they parted to draw breath, indicating his near-naked torso.

"Something I learned in Russia," said Lukas, holding her close. "The best way to save a frozen person is to put them flesh to flesh with someone healthy with a normal temperature. You have to warm them up slowly, you see."

"I see," said Trixie, then, rather stupidly, "Thank you."

"Oh, Trixie," he said hoarsely, "if I had lost you...," and he bent to kiss her again.

There was a sudden knock at the door.

"Baron, sir, it's Hester Wood, may I let Juno in? She's been whining this past hour and will not stay still."

Lukas reluctantly drew away from her. He put his finger to his lips.

"Just a moment, Miss Wood," he , "Lady Beatrix is asleep. I don't want to rouse her. Let me close her bed curtains."

He carried Trixie to her bed and put her under the covers, blankets and all. He kissed her once more, and closed the bed curtain around her. Then he buttoned his waistcoat and put on his coat.

He opened the door to Hettie and Juno, then made a to-do of lighting the candles. "I didn't do this before," he said, "for fear of waking her."

With the bed curtains closed, Trixie apparently asleep and the candles lit, the room showed every evidence of the Baron having been sitting alone by the fire.

"Once Lady Beatrix stopped shivering," he continued, adopting a detached tone, "and I could perceive no further ill effects, I put her into her bed. But I had considerable experience of the effects of the cold on the human body during Bonaparte's Russian campaign and I know an apparent recovery can be misleading. I therefore stayed to make sure she was not going to slip into unconsciousness. That is a possibility when a victim of the cold stops shivering, you know. But I am almost sure her ladyship will be perfectly well when she wakes up."

Juno had meanwhile limped into the room and over to the bed. She whined and tried to scratch at the bed covers with her injured paw.

"I see you are doing better, Juno," said Lukas. "I suppose there is no harm in letting you see your savior."

He parted the curtain, picked up the dog and placed her next to Trixie. Juno scuffled upward until her nose was next to Trixie's face. Then she gave her an encouraging lick on the cheek.

Trixie opened her eyes. "Oh, Juno," she said, as if waking up, and bringing a white arm out from under the covers to pat her. "I thought you might die! I'm so sorry." She looked up at Lukas and tears came to her eyes, "I'm so sorry about everything!"

"Miss Wood," said the Baron, "may I trouble you to bring Lady Beatrix up another cup of tea? Hot this time."

"Of course, sir," Hettie bustled away.

As soon as the door was closed, Lukas took a weeping Trixie into his arms. He held her until her sobbing stopped.

"I'm sorry, too. Trixie," he said into her hair. It had dried into wild curls. "Sorry for criticizing your faults and not appreciating your wonderful qualities, sorry for driving you away from me, sorry for not telling you before how much I love you."

He kissed her again and she returned his embrace passionately, oblivious to the impropriety of being in her bed, alone with a man and practically naked. It was perhaps fortunate that Hettie interrupted them, calling from outside, "I have the hot tea, sir."

Lukas went to the door and opened it.

"Margarethe is asking if she may come up, sir," said Hettie, bustling in. "She's so anxious about poor Trixie."

"I'll go and tell her she may." He smiled lovingly at Beatrix and left them.

Chapter Forty-Nine

With Hettie's aid, Trixie put on her nightgown and robe. They both helped Juno down from the high bed and she limped over to lie by the fire. Margarethe arrived and the three ladies sat together discussing the frightful events of the day.

"It was all my fault," said Trixie shaking her head. "I wouldn't listen to anyone. Why am I so pigheaded? And poor Juno! She was horribly wounded. It was a fox trap. Awful! So much blood! I was sure she was dying!"

"But Lukas says she owes you her life and Smithers says you saved her leg by splinting and bandaging it," reported Margarethe. "He says he doesn't know how you ever did it, and how you got the trap off in the first place. It usually takes a strong man."

"I knew I had to, and I was determined. I used branches of wood from the sheep pens. That's how I cut my hands. Thank you for bandaging them, whoever did."

Lukas had come into the room. He heard Beatrix's explanation.

"So you were determined. Now that's a surprise!" he said coming towards her with a smile. "I can only hope that when we're married you are as determined to look after me." He pulled her gently to her feet. "You will marry me, Trixie, won't you? Not because of any stupid convention, but because you want to and because I love and need you."

"Oh yes, Trixie!" cried Margarethe. "You must! You are the perfect wife for him, and the perfect sister for me!"

"Yes indeed," said Hettie. "Do you remember, Trixie, before we met the dear Baron, we were talking about how you would need to respect your husband? It is impossible not to respect the Baron, you must agree."

"Yes, Hettie. You were right, as usual." She looked up into Lukas's eyes. "It's impossible not to respect the Baron. Yes, Lukas, I will marry you, I've loved you from the moment I first saw you, though I didn't realize it was love. And we need each other. I know I'm often stupidly impulsive and impatient, and you, well, once your mind is made up you're immoveable!"

"Yes, but with your determination and my patience, it will work."

"What do you mean, your *patience*?" cried Trixie. "You are as bad as I am!"

Lukas laughed and pulled her close.

"I'm sorry," she said, looking contritely up at him, I should have listened to you about going out for a walk with bad weather coming. I shouldn't immediately want to do the opposite of what anyone says, and I should be able to control myself. I realize now that the only way you could survive the terrible times you've lived through was by exercising an absolute will. I don't have the excuse you have."

"With you by my side, I think I'll be able to control myself, too," replied Lukas softly. "Things will be better." He smiled into her eyes, then spoke louder. "You will forgive me, ladies," he said to his sister and Hettie, "but Lady Beatrix could suffer a relapse at any minute. It's essential I keep her body temperature up."

He held Trixie close and kissed her long and hard.

Margarethe clapped her hands delightedly, Hettie blushed, and from the hearth Juno looked on approvingly.

At last, she said to herself. *They certainly took their time. Silly animals.*

If you enjoyed this novel, please leave a review! Reviews are very important for novelists! Please use the link or the QR Code to scroll down the Amazon page to the Review field on the left.

https://www.amazon.com/gp/product/B0BCD2DYTM?ref_=dbs

Regency Novels by GL Robinson

Please go to my Amazon Author Page for more information:

Regency Titles

Imogen or Love and Money Lovely young widow Imogen is pursued by Lord Ivo, a well-known rake. She angrily rejects him and concentrates on continuing her late husband's business enterprises. But will she find that love is more important than money?

Cecilia or Too Tall to Love Orphaned Cecilia, too tall and too outspoken for acceptance by the *ton*, is determined to open a school for girls in London's East End slums, but is lacking funds. When Lord Tommy Allenby offers her a way out, will she get more than she bargained for?

Rosemary or Too Clever to Love Governess Rosemary is forced to move with her pupil, the romantically-minded Marianne, to live with the girl's guardian, a strict gentleman with old fashioned ideas about young women should behave. Can she save the one from her own folly and persuade the other that she isn't just a not-so-pretty face?

The Kissing Ball A collection of Regency short stories, not just for Christmas. All sorts of seasons and reasons!

The Earl and The Mud-Covered Maiden *The House of Hale Book One.* When a handsome stranger covers her in mud driving too fast and then lies about his name, little does Sophy know her world is about to change forever.

The Earl and His Lady *The House of Hale Book Two.* Sophy and Lysander are married, but she is unused to London society and he's very proud of his family name. It's a rocky beginning for both of them.

The Earl and The Heir *The House of Hale Book Three.* The Hale family has a new heir, in the shape of Sylvester, a handful of a little boy with a lively curiosity. His mother is curious too, about her husband's past. They both get themselves in a lot of trouble.

The Lord and the Red-Headed Hornet Orphaned Amelia talks her way into a man's job as secretary to a member of the aristocracy. She's looking for a post in the Diplomatic Service for her twin brother. But he wants to join the army. And her boss goes missing on the day he is supposed to show up for a wager. Can feisty Amelia save them both?

The Lord and the Bluestocking The Marquess of Hastings is good-looking and rich but a little odd. Nowadays he would probably be diagnosed as having Asperger's syndrome. To find a wife he scandalizes the ton by advertising in the newspaper. Elisabeth Maxwell is having no luck finding a publisher for her children's book and is willing to marry him to escape an overbearing stepfather. This gently amusing story introduces us to an unusual but endearing Regency couple. The question is: can they possibly co-exist, let alone find happiness?

The Lord and the Cat's Meow A love tangle between a Lord, a retired Colonel, a lovely debutante, and a fierce animal rights activist. But Horace the cat knows what he wants. He sorts it out.

Héloise Says No The lovely and mysterious Héloise is available... for a price. The Earl of Dexter is prepared to pay it, and more, but she refuses him. Told against the background of a family fleeing the French Revolution making its way the best it can, this story, by turns humorous and serious, celebrates a strong woman who will do whatever she must to ensure a safe future for those she loves.

About The Author

GL Robinson is a retired French professor. She dedicates all her books to her sister, who died unexpectedly in 2018 and who, like her, had a lifelong love of the Regency Romance genre. She remembers the two of them reading Georgette Heyer after lights out under the covers in their convent boarding school and giggling together in delicious complicity.

Brought up in the south of England, she has spent the last forty years in the Northeast USA with her American husband, children and grandchildren. She still reads Georgette Heyer.

Printed in Great Britain
by Amazon